BURNING THE
GASPEE

BURNING THE GASPEE

REVOLUTION IN RHODE ISLAND

RORY RAVEN

THE
History
PRESS

Published by The History Press
Charleston, SC 29403
www.historypress.net

Copyright © 2012 by Rory Raven
All rights reserved

Cover image courtesy of the Rhode Island Historical Society. *The Burning of the* Gaspee, 1772. Charles deWolf Brownell. RI. 1892. Oil on canvas, Rhi X5 10.

First published 2012

Manufactured in the United States

ISBN 978.1.60949.478.0

Library of Congress CIP data applied for.

Notice: The information in this book is true and complete to the best of our knowledge. It is offered without guarantee on the part of the author or The History Press. The author and The History Press disclaim all liability in connection with the use of this book.

All rights reserved. No part of this book may be reproduced or transmitted in any form whatsoever without prior written permission from the publisher except in the case of brief quotations embodied in critical articles and reviews.

In memory of George Bandel,
A teacher who knew that education was
"Lighting a fire and not filling a pail."

Contents

Acknowledgements

No one writes a book on his own—at least, I don't. The following were all of great help in this project, and all deserve gratitude beyond what a simple shout-out on an acknowledgements page can provide:

My wife, Judith Reilly, who puts up with a lot. And I do mean a lot.

Henry A.L. Brown, a Brown family descendant and a new friend, who was incredibly helpful and generous with his time and knowledge.

Alison Bundy from the Hay Library at Brown, who is always a great help.

Mike Chandley of Cellar Stories Bookstore, who always knows who I should talk to.

Larry dePetrillo, historian and collector, was supportive and enthusiastic from the start.

The Gaspee Days Committee that maintains the vast and obsessively detailed Gaspee Virtual Archives at www.gaspee.org. Webmaster Dr. John Concannon was helpful and pointed me in the right direction several times.

Kle Hall was supportive and helpful with British Royal Navy trivia.

Jill Jann, for enthusiasm and support and one of my favorite laughs ever.

Brian McCarty, who could call a little more often. Just saying.

Favorite neighbor John McNiff helped once again, this time by sorting out nautical esoterica.

The staffs of the RI Historical Society Library (I'm looking at you, Natasha), the John Hay Library of Brown University and the Providence Public Library were helpful in tracking down various items and images.

Likewise, my splendid Kickstarter backers all displayed conspicuous valor for their help in defraying usurious historic image licensing fees:

Susanne Bohne Bencivenga, still lovely after all these years.

Scott Bonelli (www.bigheadstudio.com), who contributed just to screw with the math.

Naomi Cummings, the adorable Kevin and the equally adorable Paul. It's an adorable family, really.

Anna Bouley, a supportive friend of a friend.

Amy Lynn Budd (www.riburlesqueacademy.com), who is just marvelous beyond words.

Jennifer Canole, whom I remember when she was an intern.

The excellent Daniel Ciora, onboard once again.

Alexander Davis, a supportive stranger. Thank you!

Betty Dion, yet another supportive friend of a friend.

Faye Dvorchak, who is charming and lovely in equal measure.

Jacob Haller (music.jwgh.org), a talented singer/songwriter.

Sheila Hallisey, who is always good company.

Ricky Laprade, a filmmaker you should keep an eye on.

Sarah Lewis, who threw her support behind the wayward colonists on this project.

Nicky Mariani, who bakes pies, runs marathons, has impeccable taste in '80s music and stage manages like nobody's business.

Christopher Martin, keeper of the definitive RI website, www.quahog.org.

Taylar McRee, from the old days at the Castle.

Bethany Nicholson, whom I like despite her association with that "other" tour.

Frank O'Donnell (www.frankocomedy.net), who is as nice as he is hilarious. Thanks, big man.

James Quinn, whom I've never met, but any friend of Frank's is a friend of mine.

Sheila Quinn, my favorite oldest sister.

Paul Ramsay (www.paulramsay.com), whom I don't get to hang with often enough these days.

William Schaff, who is a great friend and an even better artist, who helped out with images and turned me on to Kickstarter to begin with.

Scratch and Mina (www.bostonbabydolls.net), master and mistress of the Boston Babydolls.

Kate Eileen Shannon—watch for her Brigid Kildare mysteries.

The fine folks at the Spot Underground (www.thespotprovidence.com), thanks for thinking of me.

Kathleen Standard and Rick Vorndran, fans, friends, chauffeurs and generally nice, supportive people.

Chapter 1

ROGUE'S ISLAND

Ahandful of longboats glided across the water on a moonless night. The men—some at the oars, others nervously fingering muskets or clubs or handspikes—were silent as they drew closer and closer to the silhouette of a schooner a short distance away. A white British ensign fluttered from the schooner's topmast in a humid breeze.

A sentry on deck peered into the darkness, catching sight of the approaching boats.

"Who comes there?" he called.

The men in the boats bristled at the sentry's English accent.

"We mean to come aboard," replied a big man in the lead boat.

"You cannot," the sentry shouted back. "You cannot come aboard."

A moment later, the schooner's commanding officer came on deck. Roused from his bunk, he stood at the rail in his shirtsleeves. Raising a pistol, he warned the men to come no closer.

Another man in another boat rose to his feet and declared, "I am the sheriff of the county of Kent, God damn you. I have a warrant to apprehend you, God damn you. So surrender, God damn you!"

The officer drew his sword and repeated his warning. Some of the sailors under his command joined him, weapons at the ready.

Burning the *Gaspee*, from *Harper's New Monthly Magazine*, August 1883. *Courtesy Henry A.L. Brown.*

In one of the boats, a man turned to the friend seated next to him, saying, "Reach me your gun—I can kill that fellow."

The gun was handed over. Shouldering the musket, the man took aim, and the shot echoed across the waters.

The officer doubled over and fell.

"I am done for!" he rasped, as blood stained the deck.

With a loud cry of triumph, the men pulled hard at their oars, and the boats shot forward.

Panic erupted on deck as they clambered over the rails and swarmed the helpless schooner. The surprised crew grappled with the raiders, and suddenly, a big man loomed over the stricken officer.

"Let me dispatch this piratical dog," he cried, hefting a handspike.

Behind him, the raiders were tying up the crew and shoving them into the longboats.

A short time later, someone caught a whiff of smoke from somewhere…

Rhode Islanders have been unruly from the very beginning. Roger Williams, the puritan theologian and firebrand, founded Providence in 1636 after being banished from the Massachusetts Bay Colony for his "diverse new and dangerous opinions." Those opinions included such radical ideas as the strict separation of church and state and fair treatment of the local Indian tribes. Asserting that "forced worship stinks in God's nostrils," Williams dedicated his new settlement to "soul liberty," and the town and the colony that grew up around it became a haven for freethinkers, dissenters and those whose beliefs made them unwelcome elsewhere. The growing population of spiritual misfits drew the contempt of the Puritan colonies surrounding them. Cotton Mather dismissed Rhode Island with a sneer, calling it "the sewer of New England."

The freedoms that Rhode Islanders so prized—both religious and secular—were soon enshrined in the royal charter of 1663. Negotiated by Dr. John Clarke of Newport and granted by the court of King Charles II, the charter allowed a level of autonomy that was truly remarkable for the time. It established religious freedom in the colony, declaring that all shall "enjoy his and their own judgments and consciences, in matters of religious concernments." It went on to uphold Indian land claims and provided a blueprint for colonial government, including the election of officials—unusual in a time when most colonial officials were appointed by the Crown. Rhode Island historian Thomas Bicknell called the charter "the grandest instrument of human liberty ever constructed."

With religious freedom guaranteed and democratic government in place, Rhode Islanders turned their attention to more mundane questions, such as making money. With the thin, rocky soil, farming was never going to be as successful in the colony as it would be elsewhere, so Rhode Islanders took advantage of Narragansett Bay and turned instead to shipping and then manufacturing. Soon, those rugged philosophical individualists began to share space with Yankee traders and sea captains—hard-eyed, tight-fisted men who were every bit as fiercely independent but in a much more worldly way. These men didn't shy away from some of the more questionable ways of turning a profit.

While more successful than most others, Bristol's Simeon Potter is one example of this new breed. A self-made man, Potter's sole aim in life was to make money. "I would plow the sea into pea-porridge to make money," he once declared. An able seaman, in 1744 he sailed out of Newport Harbor as the twenty-four-year-old captain of the privateer *Prince Charles of Lorraine*, one of thousands of private citizens authorized by the British Crown to attack French targets as part of King George's War. With the privateers being awarded over half the value of the ships they captured as prizes, it could be a lucrative, if dangerous, career.

Potter threw himself into privateering with an enthusiasm that bled over into ruthlessness. Upon reaching French Guiana, he lost no time in overtaking a French fort there. Taking a musket ball in the arm did not prevent him from sacking the surrounding town and plundering it over the course of several days. He and his men even looted the church, making off with the silver, and took the brass locks and hinges from the houses. It is no surprise that the British viewed him as little more than a pirate, but at least he was their pirate.

When a British officer suggested that Potter join the Royal Navy, saying that the king would undoubtedly give him a bigger and better ship, Potter scoffed, "When I wish for a better ship, I will not ask His Majesty for one—I will build one myself!"

His privateering career was so successful that he could soon retire from it, returning to settle down in his hometown of Bristol with a fortune of a quarter of a million dollars, making him the richest man in town. He attended and supported St. Michael's Church and, in 1752, was elected to the General Assembly. A man who hated to part with his money, Potter protested tax increases by boycotting assembly meetings. He also branched out into slave trading and distilling rum—businesses that went hand in hand.

Newport alone was home to over twenty distilleries, and there were numerous "still houses" in Providence and elsewhere throughout the colony as well, all making rum for the Triangle Trade. Slave merchants, often known as "rum men," brought gallons of it to the western coast of Africa, where it was bartered for slaves. Packing one hundred or more hapless Africans into the ship's dark, stinking hold, they were transported to the West Indies on the second leg of the triangle—the infamous Middle Passage. Slaves were then sold or traded for more molasses, which, along with the remaining slaves, was brought back to Rhode Island, where the slaves would be auctioned off and the molasses sold to the distilleries, starting the whole cycle over again.

The potential profits from each leg of the journey could be huge, but entering the slave trade could be risky, to say nothing of the utter inhumanity of the entire enterprise. Nicholas Brown & Co.—the company owned by Providence brothers John, Moses, Nicholas and Joseph—sent out its first slave ship, the *Sally*, in 1764. While numbers vary from source to source, the crew of the *Sally*, captained by Esek Hopkins, acquired approximately 150 to 200 Africans on their maiden slaving voyage. At least half of the Africans died on the return trip, with disease and starvation taking a heavy toll. Others were killed during an attempted uprising, and there were, perhaps unsurprisingly, even a few suicides. After this foray into the slave trade, disastrous in so many ways, three of the Brown brothers refused to have anything further to do with the practice; Moses Brown, years later, even became a noted abolitionist. But a few years later, John Brown outfitted a bigger ship, the *Sultan*, for another slaving voyage. The potential profits were simply too much to resist.

In 1733, Parliament passed the Molasses Act, placing a steep tax of six pence per gallon on molasses imported from non–British controlled sources. This was not intended as a serious moneymaker for the Empire but rather as a way of discouraging trade with colonial rivals, particularly the hated French, who had possessions in the West Indies, cheek by jowl with Britain's own. But the British colonies there could not produce enough molasses for the thriving New England rum trade, so merchants had to look for other suppliers, even if those suppliers were French. Smuggling contraband French molasses up Narragansett Bay in the dead of night, dodging customs officials, soon became common practice. And if sneaking past the law was too daring, the enterprising smuggler could always forge invoices claiming that the gallons of molasses in the hold had been obtained from legitimate British sources.

In 1756, tensions between Britain and France boiled over into the Seven Years' War, often considered the first true world war, as entangling alliances drew much of Europe into the conflict. In North America, this played out as the French and Indian War, as France and its Indian allies challenged Britain for control of the American colonies. Rhode Island merchants were quick to see new opportunities. War is always good for business.

One way Rhode Islanders took advantage of the situation was with "flag-of-truce" voyages. During wartime, a ship from the British colonies flying a flag of truce would be allowed to enter French ports to return French prisoners of war in exchange for British captives. While in port, the vessel's captain would stock up on molasses, his real motive for making the voyage. In at least one case, the crew of a captured French ship was divided up among a small flotilla of merchant vessels, each carrying only one or two prisoners and heading for French ports, returning the sailors and packing their holds with contraband. Knowing how lucrative these trips could be, Stephen Hopkins charged £500 to authorize a flag-of-truce voyage during his tenure as governor of the colony. Hopkins's tipsy characterization in the Edward and Stone musical *1776* underscored the governor's ties to the local rum industry.

By now, Rhode Island had a growing reputation for lawlessness among the other colonies—it was often condemned as "Rogue's Island"—and the practice of trading with the enemy drew harsh criticism and accusations of prolonging the war.

In England, politician William Pitt fumed at the "illegal and most pernicious trade, by which the enemy is supplied with provisions, whereby they are principally, if not alone, able to sustain and protract this long expensive war."

The Massachusetts governor complained to the British Board of Trade that "these practices will never be put an end to until Rhode Island is reduced to the subjection of the British Empire, of which at present it is no more a part than the Bahama Islands were when they were inhabited by buccaneers."

The Molasses Act expired in 1763, the same year the Seven Years' War ended. William Pitt's sharp leadership had not only won the war but also doubled the national debt. Britain needed to raise funds to pay off the debt and introduced the Sugar Act, a revamped version of the Molasses Act, reducing the tax on foreign molasses and sugar by half; it hoped that lowering the tax would get the colonists to simply pay it rather than continue their elaborate smuggling practices. And if the revised tax did not put an end to the rampant smuggling, the British also redoubled their efforts at customs enforcement, intending to prosecute anyone caught breaking the law. They attempted to further raise revenue by passing the Stamp Act, which required an official tax stamp to be purchased and placed on a wide variety of paper goods—legal documents, playing cards, magazines and newspapers and other everyday articles.

With the end of the French and Indian War, loyalty in the American colonies was higher than it had been in some time. Mother England had just gone to war to defend her far-flung children, and by and large the colonists felt more British than ever. Parliament must have thought that they would willingly pay the new taxes and, as loyal British subjects, shoulder their part of the burden.

Parliament was wrong.

·

Chapter 2

TAXATION WITHOUT REPRESENTATION

In the colonies, the new taxes met with serious resistance. Taxes collected as part of trade regulation was one thing, but these new taxes were unacceptable, especially as the colonists had no say in their implementation. Parliament had passed the Sugar and Stamp Acts, and Parliament, at least in theory, represented the will and interests of the British people. But the American colonists, half a world away, had no one representing them in Parliament, no voice in the decisions affecting them, and they balked at the new taxes. The fact that no new taxes were enacted in Britain itself, but only in the American colonies, added insult to injury. The now-familiar rallying cry of "No Taxation Without Representation" was heard for the first time.

While the Sugar Act reduced the tax on foreign-sourced molasses to three pence per gallon, half of what it had been previously, that was still not low enough for the rum men. But it was the Stamp Act that sparked the most ire.

One Howard Johnston was appointed stamp master and put in charge of implementing the new law requiring tax stamps on various items. He resigned when he and two other well-known local Tories were hanged in effigy in downtown Newport. The Tories' homes were ransacked. Afterward, crates of tax stamps sat unopened and were not even loaded off the ship lying at anchor in the harbor, as the governor shrugged innocently and said he could find no one to replace Johnston.

When a county court clerk punctiliously refused to conduct official business without the proper tax stamps in place, an angry mob gathered outside his home. Only the intercession of peacemaker Moses Brown kept things from escalating into outright violence.

The Quartering Act proved to be almost equally as unpopular. This law required colonists to supply (at their own expense) barracks and supplies to support British troops stationed within the colony. Once again, colonists chafed at having such burdens placed on them while having no say in the matter.

Stephen Hopkins penned a pamphlet entitled "The Rights of the Colonies Examined." In it, he praised the "glorious constitution" of English law while damning taxation without representation. "By this most beneficent compact British subjects are to governed only agreeable to laws to which themselves have some way consented," he wrote, adding that "those who are governed at the will of another, or of others, and whose property may be taken from them by taxes or otherwise without their own consent and against their will, are in the miserable condition of slaves."

The British continued their crackdown on smuggling, assigning several ships to drop anchor in Narragansett Bay and enforce customs regulations. They were not given a warm welcome.

The *Squirrel*, a twenty-gun warship carrying a crew of 160, arrived in Newport in 1764. (One of the difficulties in having the biggest navy on the planet is that you begin to run out of intimidating ship names; the Royal Navy had ships named the *Flirt*, the *Clown* and the *Wallflower*, among others.) She was there for the "suppression of the clandestine trade with foreign nations and the improvement of the revenue." She was soon joined by the *St. John*, an eight-gun schooner. British ships of the period were usually defined in terms of their rigging and the number of cannon they carried. Schooners were smaller, lighter, two-masted vessels, and the *St. John* was the *Squirrel*'s "ship's tender," meaning it was assigned to "attend" to the large ship by ferrying passengers or cargo to and from the warship and performing other tasks as ordered.

THE

RIGHTS

OF

COLONIES

EXAMINED.

PUBLISHED BY AUTHORITY.

By Stephen Hopkins Gov

PROVIDENCE:
PRINTED BY *WILLIAM GODDARD.*
M.DCC.LXV.

Stephen Hopkins's "Rights of Colonies Examined" first appeared as a long article in the *Providence Gazette* and was later reprinted as a pamphlet by order of the General Assembly. In it, Hopkins wrote, "We believe no good reason can be given why the colonies should not modestly and soberly inquire what right the Parliament of Great Britain have to tax them." *Courtesy the Rhode Island Historical Society. 1764. Ink on Paper. Rhi X3 4291.*

The following July, some men from the *St. John* were ashore where, according to the local newspaper, the *Newport Mercury*, they engaged in "some irregularities in town." The "irregularities" may have been an attempt to impress some Newporters into service in the Royal Navy. While most Americans associate the practice of impressment with the War of 1812, it was official British Royal Navy practice beginning in 1664 and was an unofficial practice going back much further. Life at sea was not always a happy one in the Royal Navy. In a quote often mistakenly attributed to Winston Churchill, it consisted of "rum, buggery, and the lash," and unsurprisingly, captains sometimes found themselves short of a full crew. Their answer was to send out a "press gang" to capture a number of able-bodied men and force them into service aboard a vessel.

Generally, a press gang would be on the lookout for anyone with seafaring experience, but in wartime, anyone would do.

One of the sailors in the *St. John*'s press gang was left behind that night and taken into custody, but he soon escaped, and his shipmates returned to reclaim him. They were met dockside by an angry mob, and again according to the *Mercury*, a "smart skirmish was the consequence" and "the schooner's men were considerably bruised, and very expeditiously went off." The people of Newport demanded that the offending sailors be handed over, but the British refused. The *St. John* carried the men away, heading across the harbor to join the *Squirrel*, seeking the safety of the bigger ship's twenty cannon. As the *St. John* passed Fort George on Goat Island, she was signaled to stop but ignored the warning, and the men of the fort, under orders to keep the schooner confined to the harbor, fired on her. According to a plaque on the island:

> *By order of Governor Stephen Hopkins and members of the Rhode Island General Assembly, thirteen 18-pounder cannon shots were fired from Fort George on this spot at the British Navy's 8-gun schooner St. John on July 9, 1764 in order to protect Newport's principal industry, smuggling. The St. John, moderately damaged, quickly sailed away from Newport. These were the first shots in resistance to British authority in America, leading directly to the American Revolution.*

Another British ship, the twenty-eight-gun frigate *Maidstone*, ran afoul of the colonists in 1765. When her captain impressed a number of Newport men, the governor demanded their immediate release. The *Maidstone*'s captain of course refused, but a mob caught one of his officers ashore and gave the man a beating. Cutting loose a longboat belonging to the *Maidstone*—presumably this was the one that brought the officer ashore and was still tied up at the dock—the mob dragged the boat through the streets of Newport and burned it in front of the Colony House.

In Providence, an overzealous customs official, a "tidewaiter," was tarred and feathered one night on the waterfront.

The plaque on Goat Island commemorating the attack on the *St. John* in 1764. *Author's collection.*

Tensions continued to mount, and a few years later, colonists meted out even harsher punishment to the *Liberty*, yet another British warship hunting for contraband. The *Liberty* had originally belonged to John Hancock, then a successful Boston businessman whose hobby seemed to be evading the Townshend duties and thumbing his nose at the British authorities. Customs officials eventually seized the *Liberty* on suspicion of smuggling wine, and while the charges against Hancock were eventually dropped, the British refused to return the ship to him.

In 1769, refitted as an armed sloop and under the command of William Reid, the *Liberty*, now a British customs vessel, seized two ships, a brig and a sloop, off the Connecticut coast. Reid brought the ships to Newport. According to the *Newport Mercury*, he had made the seizures "on suspicion of the brig's having done some illicit act, and that the sloop had contraband goods on board." While nothing suspicious was found, the two ships were still held for several days by customs officials.

Captain Packwood, the brig's commanding officer, went to his impounded vessel to retrieve his sword and a change of clothes, but an officer from the *Liberty*, guarding the two ships, would not let him aboard. The sequence of events here is not entirely clear, because Packwood is next described as brandishing his sword at the officer, who had blocked his path and "offer'd him violence." The officer had several armed men with him. Outnumbered, Packwood put back to shore as the British sailors opened fire on him with muskets and pistols, and their shots "went very near but did not hurt him."

The next night, "a number of persons, unknown," attacked the *Liberty* when only the mate was aboard and the rest of the crew had gone ashore. They "sent the mate away" and proceeded to vandalize the ship, cutting her mooring cables and letting her drift into the shallows, where they scuttled her, even chopping down the mainmast. The irate colonists then carried two of her longboats into town and burned them, something that was now almost becoming a tradition in Newport.

In the confusion, the captured sloop made good her escape, slipping away into the night. The brig was cleared of charges, obtained the proper papers and set sail the next day. The *Liberty* sat aground off Goat Island until a person or persons unknown set fire to her a day or two later. The governor promised a full investigation into the whole sorry affair but never so much as lifted a finger after.

Whatever had passed for relations, or even tolerance, between colonists and British officials was breaking down. Tempers were fraying on both sides. It was only a matter of time before something more serious happened.

In February 1772, another British vessel dropped anchor in Narragansett Bay—the eight-gun schooner *Gaspee,* under the command of Lieutenant William Dudingston.

Everything that had gone before was simply a dress rehearsal for what happened next.

Chapter 3

HEARTS OF OAK

The *Gaspee* was originally built as a single-masted sloop. No authenticated images of the vessel survive, but she was likely a trim little craft, sixty or seventy feet long, with a crew of about twenty. It is generally agreed that she was named for the Gaspe Peninsula in New Brunswick, so she may have been built in a Canadian shipyard. She was purchased in New York for £500, one of a small batch of ships the British Royal Navy acquired for use in customs enforcement at the time. Not long after purchase, she was refitted; a second mast was added, converting her into a schooner. British Royal Navy records show that she was refitted several times, including once in Rhode Island in 1767. "Refitting" could mean anything from minor repairs to major modifications, so there is at least an outside chance that she was converted from sloop to schooner in Rhode Island, though we don't know for certain, as the records aren't that specific.

Schooners were a North American invention, swift fore-and-aft-rigged ships with a (comparatively) shallow draft, meaning they did not sit too low in the water. They were not designed to be serious oceangoing vessels, intended rather to stay close to shore or patrol narrow, shallow waterways that larger vessels could not reach. Their fore-and-aft rigging allowed them to sail in heavier weather than the big square-rigged ships.

The British Royal Navy rated its ships according to the number of cannon the ship carried. A first-rate ship, the largest, was the most heavily armed, sporting one hundred or more cannon on three gun decks. A sixth-rate ship carried twenty to twenty-four guns. Vessels with fewer than twenty guns, such as the *Gaspee*, with eight, were considered "unrated" and were usually under the command of a lieutenant rather than a captain.

While modern historians often refer to her as HMS *Gaspee* (His Majesty's Ship *Gaspee*), this is probably not how she was officially known at the time. While the HMS prefix was occasionally used for Royal Navy ships of the period, it was not as commonly used then as it would become later. Firsthand accounts refer to her variously as His Majesty's armed schooner, His Majesty's revenue schooner and even His Britannic Majesty's schooner *Gaspee*. It seems likely that, in her day, she was simply known as the *Gaspee*.

Earlier in her history, with one Thomas Allen as her master and commander, the *Gaspee* plied up and down the northeast Atlantic coast, from as far north as Halifax all the way down to Philadelphia. She intercepted smugglers, escorted a shipment of tax stamps, and acted as a ship's tender to larger vessels. A busy, if unremarkable, career.

Lieutenant Allen was discharged, and on September 13, 1768, Lieutenant William Dudingston took command of the *Gaspee*. Dudingston was a lowland Scot hailing from Fife, across the Firth of Forth from Edinburgh, on Scotland's east coast. We know almost nothing of his career before he was made master and commander of the *Gaspee*, his first command, sometime in his thirties. But if he followed a typical career path, he would have gone to sea as the onboard servant of an officer before he was even a teenager. After a few years, he would have moved from simply being referred to as a "boy" to being rated as a "midshipman." Midshipmen were officers in training who divided their time between their studies of navigation and seamanship and their onboard duties, such as keeping watch, running errands and rigging sails. After at least six years at sea, and at an age of twenty (though sometimes younger), a midshipman sat for his lieutenant's exam. The examination board consisted of a number of experienced captains. It was an oral exam, and the questions were not standardized, so the captains might be more lenient with a candidate who had connections (there is no indication that Dudingston was so connected). Midshipmen who failed their exams were never promoted and were often portrayed as bitter, hard-drinking men begrudging of others' success. Those who passed the exam were promoted to lieutenant and, if they were lucky (or connected), might be given a chance to further prove their worth by being given command of a smaller, unrated vessel, as Dudingston was with the *Gaspee*.

Once he had his command, Dudingston set about making a name for himself. And not a particularly good one. He "maltreated" a fisherman on the Delaware River, clapping the man in irons for some unspecified infraction. The fisherman sued him for "ill treatment." The *Newport Mercury* for July 17, 1769, reprinting dispatches from the Philadelphia area, referred to Dudingston as "cowardly, insolent" and even condemned him as "a disgrace to his commission."

In February 1772, Dudingston and the *Gaspee* were posted to Newport to assist in customs enforcement. We can imagine that he may not have been particularly happy about his new assignment. He may have gone to sea with dreams of becoming the empire's next great naval hero—another Sir Francis Drake. Now he found himself chasing rum smugglers around Narragansett Bay. It must have stung, and he vented his frustrations on the colonists.

The day after his arrival in Newport, Dudingston went ashore to meet with Governor Joseph Wanton. A Newport native, the sixty-seven-year-old Wanton came from a political family; his father and uncle had both been governor of the colony before him. A portrait of him hanging in Newport's Redwood Library shows a well-fed patrician in a curly wig and scarlet coat, but a sharp mind lay behind that foppish exterior, along with a more rough-and-tumble history than might be expected. He had been a rum and slave merchant, voyaging to Africa himself and being captured by a French privateer. He is often dismissed as a Loyalist, but in reality, his position was more delicate, as he walked a political tightrope between the British authorities on one side and the needs of Rhode

A nineteenth-century engraving of Newport's Colony House, the center of local government, which doubled as the customs house. *Courtesy Newport Historical Society.*

Island colonists on the other. He knew that neither side would hesitate to back up its point of view with force.

We aren't sure where their meeting took place, possibly at the Colony House in downtown Newport, but Dudingston presented himself to explain that he was here under orders from Admiral John Montagu, commander in chief of the North American station, "to assist in the revenue."

"Is it the schooner Captain Allen commanded?" Wanton asked. The *Gaspee* had been in Newport at least twice before under the command of Dudingston's predecessor, and Wanton clearly remembered.

Dudingston said yes, it was.

"We have had so many schooners here lately," Wanton said with a sigh. "The *Sultana*, the *Halifax*, the *St. John*…" He must have smiled as he mentioned the last.

Dudingston, looking for common ground, said that he had met the governor two years before in Newport, in the company of some other British military officers. He could not later recall what Wanton had said in reply.

They briefly discussed the attack upon the *Liberty* a few years before. Wanton shook his head, saying it was well within Lieutenant Reid's power to have saved the *Liberty* before she was scuttled. In Wanton's mind, no one was more to blame for the whole episode than Reid himself.

"I have heard it otherwise mentioned," Dudingston retorted, adding, "But I hope I should meet with no difficulty in the execution of my duty."

"You may depend upon my support and assistance," Wanton replied with the noncommittal tact of a career politician.

Remembering that the brig captured by the *Liberty* had gotten away in the confusion, Dudingston asked if any prizes he seized would be safe in port, or would they also mysteriously go missing?

"I will do all in my power," Wanton said blandly, seeming to have grown bored with the interview.

Dudingston replied, "I do not think if I made one [the seizure of a vessel] I should put it to the trial." He'd keep his own watch rather than trust customs officials in Newport.

"I suppose you will be much here," Wanton said as Dudingston rose to go. "I shall always be glad to see you."

"I shall be where I find I can best execute the service," the lieutenant answered. "I am much obliged to you."

"I hope, captain, we shall have a good understanding," Wanton said. Dudingston said that was also his wish, adding that he would give the governor as little trouble as possible.

(It is a long-standing tradition to refer to the master of any vessel as its "captain." So while Dudingston carried the rank of lieutenant, he probably would have been referred to as "captain" out of courtesy, rather than as a designation or acknowledgement of rank.)

Bad weather kept the *Gaspee* in port for a few days, but when the skies cleared and the waters calmed, the *Gaspee* and her commander set to work. Dudingston hired a local man named Daggett, an experienced pilot familiar with the Rhode Island coastline, its rivers and inlets and hidden coves. Knowing that smugglers sometimes offloaded contraband into smaller boats that ferried the goods quietly ashore, Dudingston began stopping every vessel he saw, from rowboats to ferries to cargo ships. He

Highlights of the *Gaspee* story. *Courtesy the Rhode Island Historical Society. From a watercolor by W.L. Greene. The Burning of the Gaspee. RI. 1898. Ink on paper. RHi X3 5372.*

would order any passing ship or boat to stop by firing off a signal cannon, and anyone who did not submit to a search would be chased down and boarded by force.

While other British customs vessels had mostly confined their activities to the waters around Newport, Dudingston took advantage of Daggett's local knowledge to range much farther up Narragansett Bay in search of illicit cargo than had his predecessors.

Dudingston's questionable activities continued ashore. On at least one occasion, he ordered a group of men to take several sheep from a pasture within sight of the shoreline. Mutton was served aboard the *Gaspee* that night, and the farmer who owned the sheep was outraged.

Another band of Dudingston's men went ashore at Gould Island, lying between Jamestown and Aquidneck Island, "and committed trespass and waste thereon, by cutting down thirty or more trees and carrying the same from off said island," according to the island's "proprietor," a Mr. Faulkner. The proprietor was urged to bring suit against Dudingston, but the lieutenant settled with him, paying him fifteen dollars, probably more to shut the man up than because he actually thought he was in the wrong.

However much he annoyed the colonists, he crossed the line when he seized the *Fortune*, a sloop belonging to the powerful Greene family.

Chapter 4

HATE MAIL

Nathanael Greene was a member of the Rhode Island General Assembly and a man who would go on to distinguish himself as a key general under George Washington during the Revolution. Like so many other Rhode Islanders, he had diverse business interests: he and his family owned a forge and also ran a shipping business. Nathanael did not take too active a role in shipping, leaving it mostly in the capable hands of his younger brother, Rufus.

On a cold day in March 1772, Dudingston sighted the cargo sloop *Fortune* lying at anchor off North Kingstown. He sent over a boarding party, led by his right-hand man, an officer named James Dundas. Pushing his way aboard and finding twenty-four-year-old Rufus Greene Jr. in command, Dundas ordered him to unlock the hatches so the hold might be inspected. When Rufus replied that the latches were already unlocked, Dundas evidently decided he didn't like the young man's tone and ordered him to wait in his cabin while the ship was searched. Rufus must have raised an eyebrow as he demanded to know under what authority Dundas was acting. Dundas drew his sword in answer.

"If you do not go into the cabin, I'll let you know," he warned and, grabbing Rufus by the collar, shoved him roughly into the cabin.

Leaving him there, Dundas checked the *Fortune*'s hold, where he discovered twelve hogsheads of rum. A hogshead is a large cask, and when used as a unit of measure, the amount varies from source to source; when used to hold wine, the amount varies from one type of wine to the next, so it is frustratingly difficult to tell just how much rum was stowed in the hold, but it was probably 750 gallons or so.

The rum, the Jamaican spirits and the barrel of brown sugar beside it all lacked the proper paperwork, the *Fortune* having skirted customs in Newport. Dundas must have smiled in triumph as he gave the order to seize the vessel for smuggling.

Rufus Greene had slipped out of the cabin while Dundas and his men conducted their search, and now Dundas "clenched upon" him, throwing him back into the cabin, where he "jammed the companion leaf upon his head." The companion leaf is the door to the companionway, a narrow flight of stairs leading between decks. This seems to be a common occurrence; there are several accounts of scuffles aboard various ships that end with someone getting smacked with the companion leaf. Rufus remained confined "for a considerable time" as Dundas took charge of the *Fortune*, marking her hatches with an "R" to indicate the sloop had been seized, and towing her to Newport.

Rufus was brought before Dudingston. He once again demanded to know under what authority these actions were being performed. Did the *Gaspee*'s commander even have a commission (i.e., written orders) to make such a seizure? Dudingston simply said that he had a good commission from His Majesty and ordered Rufus confined. He was transferred to another ship the following day and then apparently released from there.

Normally, if an officer seized a vessel on a charge of smuggling, the case would be heard by the local vice-admiralty court, a judiciary set up specifically to handle maritime cases. But any merchant appearing as a defendant before such a court knew the deck was stacked against him. Trials were decided by the judge, not a jury. There was no chance of a case being decided by a group of sympathetic peers. To make matters worse, judges were awarded a percentage of the ships and cargo whose seizure they upheld, so it comes as no surprise that the vast majority of judges found the accused guilty as charged and ordered the vessel and its cargo to be auctioned off, pocketing a portion of the proceeds in the process.

In Rhode Island, then as now, everyone seemed to know one another, and there were certain understandings in place. Even if one did not have such an understanding with the vice-admiralty judge, most merchants knew that when (and not if) they lost their case, they could depend on friends and colleagues to avoid bidding on the condemned vessel. Auction-goers would stand mute, and the boat's original owner would be the only one to enter a bid, thereby reclaiming his property. Sometimes, as Dudingston well knew, vessels didn't even get as far as the auction block, as he had mentioned to Governor Wanton during their brief interview. Sometimes seized vessels simply went missing.

The *Fortune* was Dudingston's first major seizure since his arrival in the colony. He decided not to "put it to the trial" and, taking no chances, ordered the captured sloop and its cargo to Boston for trial in that vice-admiralty court, sidestepping Rhode Island jurisdiction altogether.

This was a serious mistake. Up until now, Dudingston had simply been one more obnoxious functionary who delighted in harassing and annoying colonists. Rhode Islanders had seen others like him come and go. But turning the *Fortune* over to the Boston vice-admiralty court was a slap in the face.

The royal charter of 1663 instructed the people of Rhode Island "to appoint, order and direct, erect and settle, such places and courts of jurisdiction, for the hearing and determining of all actions, cases, matters and things, happening within the said colony and plantation, and which shall be in dispute, and depending there, as they shall think fit." Sending the *Fortune* out of the colony for trial in Boston violated the charter, which dictated that the Rhode Island courts had jurisdiction, as the seizure took place within the colony's borders. Dudingston had broken the law, and a warrant was promptly issued for his arrest. The lieutenant was forced to stay aboard the *Gaspee*, refusing to go ashore for fear of arrest.

By now, Lieutenant William Dudingston was easily the most hated man in Rhode Island. He continued to stop and search passing boats, drawing the ire of the colonists. A number of prominent citizens, Providence's

John Brown among them, complained to Chief Justice Stephen Hopkins, asking for his legal opinion on Dudingston's actions. They also aired their concerns to Deputy Governor Darius Sessions, who in turn contacted Governor Wanton.

> *Providence, March 21, 1772*
>
> *Sir:— The inhabitants of this town have, of late, been much disquieted in their minds, by repeated advices being brought of a schooner which for some time past hath cruised Narragansett Bay and much disturbed our navigation. She suffers no vessel to pass, not even packet boats, or others of an inferior kind, without a strict examination, and where any sort of unwillingness is discovered, they are compelled to submit, by an armed force. Who he is and by what authority he assumes such a conduct, it is thought, needs some inquiry…*
>
> *It is suspected that he has no legal authority to justify his conduct, and his commission, if he has any, is some antiquated paper, more of a fiction than anything else and this seems to be confirmed by Mr. Thomas Greene, who says he saw it, and believes it to be no other than the commission the famous Reid had, who lost his sloop at Newport, or something else of no validity. In consequence of the above mentioned application, I have consulted with the chief justice thereon, who is of the opinion, that no commander of any vessel has any right to use the authority in the body of the colony without previously applying to the Governor and showing his warrant for so doing and also being sworn to a due exercise of his office—and he informs me that this has been the common custom in the colony.*
>
> *I am, sir, with the greatest respect, your Honor's most obedient and humble servant,*
> *Darius Sessions.*

Wanton then fired off a letter to Dudingston, in high eighteenth-century dudgeon. To underscore how serious the matter was, he had it hand delivered aboard the *Gaspee* by the high sheriff.

NEWPORT, RHODE ISLAND.
March 22, 1772
SIR:—A considerable number of the inhabitants of this Colony have complained to me of your having, in a most illegal and unwarrantable manner, interrupted their trade, by searching and detaining every little packet boat plying between the several towns. As I know not by what authority you assume this power, I have sent off the high sheriff, to inform you of the complaint exhibited against you, and expect that you do, without delay, produce me your commission and instructions, if any you have, which was your duty to have done when you first came within the jurisdiction of this Colony.
I am your humble servant,
J. WANTON.
To the commanding officer of a schooner near Brenton's Point

Dudingston's shock, real or feigned, was palpable when he received Wanton's letter. He sent one of his men, probably Dundas, ashore with his response:

GASPEE, Rhode Island, March 23, 1772.
SIR:—Last night, I received your letter informing me that a "number of the inhabitants of this Colony had complained" to you of my having "in a most illegal and unwarrantable manner interrupted their packet boats, plying between the several towns."
In answer to which, I have done nothing but what was my duty, and their complaint can only be founded on their ignorance of that. When I waited on you, on my arrival, I acquainted you of my being sent to this government to assist the revenue. I had my commission to show you if required, as it was ever understood by all his Majesty's governors I have had the honor to wait on, that every officer commanding one of his Majesty's vessels was properly authorized and never did produce it, unasked for. The officer I send is equally qualified, and has been in the boats in boarding most of the vessels, and can give any information relative to my proceeding.

Sir, your humble servant,
W. DUDINGSTON

Wanton then dashed off another quick reply:

NEWPORT, RHODE ISLAND
MARCH 23, 1772
SIR:—Yours of this day I have received, which does not give me that
satisfaction I had a right to expect; neither was the bearer of the letter
qualified to give me any authentic information respecting the legality of
that authority you have presumed to exercise within this Colony. I expect
that you do without delay, comply with my request of yesterday, and you
may be assured that my utmost exertions shall not be wanting to protect
your person from any insult or outrage on coming ashore.
I am your humble servant,
J. WANTON.
To Mr. W. Dudingston, of the Schooner Gaspee.

We can only wonder how sincere Wanton's assurance was. He might have been only too happy to see Dudingston "outraged" like some of the interfering British officers before him.

Dudingston threw up his hands and referred the matter to his superior in Boston, Admiral Montagu. As commander in chief of the North American station, fifty-three-year-old John Montagu oversaw all British Royal Navy ships and activities on the East Coast, from Halifax to Bermuda. He had been enrolled in the first class at the Royal Navy Academy in Portsmouth, England, when it opened in 1733, eventually becoming the captain of his own ship and serving in the European theater of the Seven Years' War. By 1772, he held the rank of rear admiral of the Blue (the British Royal Navy was divided up into red, white and blue squadrons, each commanded by an admiral, a vice-admiral and a rear admiral; rear admiral is the lowest of the admiral ranks but still nothing to sneeze at).

John Adams had met Montagu and did not like him, noting in his diary the admiral's "coarse, low, vulgar dialect" and adding that "his brutal, hoggish manners are a disgrace to the Royal Navy, and the King's service." Adams didn't like the shrewish Mrs. Montagu any better, though he may have liked her better than did the admiral himself—Adams quotes Montagu as grumbling, "My wife's damned arse is so broad that she and I can't sit in a chariot [carriage] together."

Montagu entered the war of words on April 6, 1772, writing to Governor Wanton:

Boston, 6th April, 1772

Sir:—Lieutenant Dudingston, commander of his Majesty's armed schooner and a part of the squadron under my command, has sent me two letters he received from you of such a nature I am at a loss what answer to give them, and ashamed to find they come from one of his Majesty's Governors. He informs me that he waited upon you and showed you the admiralty and my orders for his proceedings, which, agreeable to his instructions, he is to do, that you may be acquainted that he is on that station to protect your province from pirates and to give the trade all the assistance he can, and to endeavor, as much as lays in his power, to protect the revenue officer, and to prevent (if possible) the illicit trade that is carrying on at Rhode Island.

He, sir, has done his duty and behaved like an officer, and it is your duty as a governor, to give him your assistance, and not endeavor to distress the King's officers for strictly complying with my orders. I shall give them directions, that, in case they receive any molestation in the execution of their duty, they shall send every man so taken in molesting them, to me. I am also informed, the people of Newport talk of fitting out an armed vessel to rescue any vessel the King's schooner may take carrying on an illicit trade. Let them be cautious what they do; for as sure as they attempt it, and any of them are taken, I will hang them as pirates. I shall report your two insolent letters to my officer, to his Majesty's Secretaries of State, and leave them to determine what right you have to demand a sight of all orders I shall give to all officers of my squadron, and I would advise you not to send your Sheriff on board the King's ship again, on such ridiculous

*errands. The Captain and Lieutenants have all my orders to give you
assistance whenever you demand it, but further you have no business
with them, and, be assured, it is not their duty to show you any part
of my orders or instructions to them.*

I am, sir, your most humble servant.

J. MONTAGU

Note that Dudingston seems to have changed his story. When writing back and forth with Wanton, he states that he had his papers with him but the governor never asked to see them and (as he states in his letter of March 23) that "every officer commanding one of His Majesty's vessels was properly authorized and never did produce it, unasked for." But he has apparently told Montagu that he did in fact produce his orders, as the admiral writes, "He informs me that he waited upon you and showed you the Admiralty and my orders for his proceedings." Someone was lying.

The situation was growing delicate. For now, at least, it seemed like little more than a diplomatic kerfuffle, a snarky exchange about an overzealous officer's conduct. Wanton didn't get back to Montagu for a month.

RHODE ISLAND, May 8, 1772.

*SIR:—Your letter dated April the 8ᵗʰ at Boston, I have received.
Lieutenant Dudingston has done well in transmitting my letters to
you, which I sent him; but I am sorry to be informed there is any
thing contained in them that should be construed as a design of giving
offence, when no such thing was intended. But Mr. Dudingston has not
behaved so well in asserting to you "he waited on me and showed me
the admiralty and your orders for his proceedings which agreeable to his
instruction he is to do," but in that he has altogether misinformed you,
for he, at no time, ever showed me any orders from the admiralty or from
you, and positively denied that he derived any authority either from you
or the commissioners; therefore, it was altogether out of my power to
know, whether he came hither to protect us from pirates, or was a pirate
himself.—You say "he has done his duty and behaved like an officer."*

In this I apprehend you must be mistaken, for I can never believe it is the duty of any officer, to give false information to his superiors. As to your attempt to point out what was my duty as Governor, please to be informed, that I do not receive instructions for the administration of my government, from the King's admiral stationed in America. You seem to assert that I have endeavored to distress the King's officer, for strictly complying with your orders. In this you are altogether mistaken, for I have at all times heretofore, and shall constantly for time to come, afford them all the aid and assistance in my power in the execution of their office. The information you have received "that the people of Newport talked of fitting out an armed vessel to rescue any vessel the King's schooner might take carrying on an illicit trade," you may be assured is without foundation, and a scandalous imposition, for upon inquiring into this matter, I cannot find that any such design was ever made, or so much as talked of, and, therefore, I hope you will not hang any of his Majesty's subjects belonging to his colony upon such false information. I am greatly obliged for the promise of transmitting my letters to the Secretary of State. I am, however, a little shocked at your impolite expression made use of upon that occasion; in return for this good office, I shall also transmit your letter to the Secretary of State, and leave to the King and his ministers to determine on which side the charge of insolence lies. As to your advice not to send the Sheriff on board any of your squadron, please to know, that I will send the Sheriff of this Colony at any time, and to any place, within the body of it, as I shall think fit. In the last paragraph of your letter you are pleased flatly to contradict what you wrote in the beginning; for there you assert that Dudingston, by his instructions, was directed to show me the admiralty and your orders to him, and here you assert, that I have no business with them, and assure me that it is not his duty to show me them or any part thereof.
I am, sir, your humble servant,
J. WANTON

Battle lines had been drawn.

Chapter 5

MUFFLED OARS

Captain Benjamin Lindsay makes a brief appearance, plays a crucial role in the story and then leaves the stage, never to return. Lindsay (sometimes spelled Lindsey) and his brother Thomas ran daily stageboats between Providence and Newport, carrying "goods and passengers." Like a stagecoach, a stageboat ran from point A to point B on a regular schedule, sometimes with stops along the route. The brothers' service was perhaps a little unusual, as "for the convenience of passengers, they propose to supply their boats with provisions and liquors of all kinds."

On June 8, 1772, Benjamin Lindsay arrived in Newport from a voyage to New York at the helm of his cargo sloop, the *Hannah*. He remained anchored in Newport Harbor overnight, filing his papers at the Colony House and receiving the necessary clearances and getting underway around noon the next day. On June 9, 1772, he sailed up Narragansett Bay, bound for Providence.

The *Hannah* was soon sighted by the *Gaspee*, and Dudingston signaled her to stop for inspection. He may have fired off a signal gun, as was common practice. But some versions of the story state that in a more blatantly belligerent move, he fired a shot across the *Hannah*'s bow.

Captain Lindsay ignored the signal and continued on his way toward Providence. We don't know why he ignored the signal, as he never made

STAGE-BOATS from *Providence* to *Newport.*

THOMAS and BENJAMIN LINDSEY beg Leave to inform the Public, That they have now three very compleat Stage-Boats, for the Carriage of Goods and PASSENGERS, which fail from PROVIDENCE and NEW-PORT every Day. For the Convenience of Paffengers, they propofe to fupply their Boats with Provifions and Liquors of all Kinds, and have provided a convenient Store for the Reception of Goods, with Conveniences for weighing the fame, at Arnold's Wharff, juft below the Sign of the Buck, in Providence. Thofe who may pleafe to favour them with their Bufinefs, may depend on being ferved with the utmoft Fidelity, and Paffengers will be treated in the moft genteel Manner. (4)

A newspaper ad for the Lindsay brothers' stageboat business. *Courtesy Henry A.L. Brown.*

a statement explaining his actions. Perhaps he felt that as he had already cleared customs in Newport, Dudingston had no business stopping him. Perhaps, like so many, he had lost all patience with the vindictive lieutenant and wouldn't give him the satisfaction of stopping. Or perhaps he feared that Dudingston would seize the *Hannah* on some pretext and send her to Boston for trial, as he had the *Fortune*.

Aboard the *Gaspee*, Dudingston, no doubt incensed by the man's insubordination, gave the order to chase down the *Hannah*. The pursuit led farther and farther up the bay. Soon, Warwick's Namquit Point was in view. Namquit (sometimes spelled Namquid) was a spit of land jutting out into the water in a spot where the bay bottlenecked down from five miles across to just under a mile. The shallows around the Point were a hazard well known to local pilots like Captain Lindsay.

Unfortunately for Dudingston, Daggett, the local pilot he had hired, had been transferred over to the *Beaver*, another British revenue ship, and was not onboard the *Gaspee* that day. The man at the helm must not have been as familiar with local waters.

Details of what exactly happened are scanty; oral history and popular imagination have filled in many of the gaps. Lindsay may have been able to steer the *Hannah* through the shallow waters of Namquit Point,

Gaspee Point today. *Author's collection.*

skimming over the treacherous sandbar lurking beneath the surface. In the heat of the chase, the *Gaspee* may have tried the same maneuver… but ran aground.

Debate continues to this day as to whether Lindsay deliberately lured the schooner into the shallow waters or if the *Gaspee* running aground was simply a happy coincidence. Either way, a cheer must have gone up on the deck of the *Hannah* as the crew realized Dudingston's predicament and the hated schooner receded in the distance. Oral tradition says men of the *Hannah* mooned the *Gaspee* crew as they left them behind.

Lindsay continued to Providence, probably weighing his options the entire way. The tide was ebbing and the *Gaspee* wasn't going anywhere until high tide—three o'clock the next morning. Chance had placed an opportunity before him and the rest of the men whom Dudingston had made so miserable over the last few months. But what to do with that opportunity?

The *Hannah* reached Providence around sunset, just as the shops were closing. Lindsay knew he needed to get the word out about the *Gaspee*'s situation. Stepping onto the dock, he knew he needed to find one of the city's leading men, one of Dudingston's most vocal critics.

He went looking for John Brown.

In a story populated by larger-than-life characters, John Brown is by far the largest. At age twelve, he had declared himself "the cleverest boy in Providence Town," and later in life, his children would call him "Old Thunder." There can be no doubt that this was a man who filled any room he was in, his tall, three-hundred-pound frame suiting his outsized personality.

Thirty-five years old in 1772, he was already one of the city's most prominent citizens. A wealthy merchant and slave trader, he had outfitted privateers during the French and Indian War and later didn't hesitate to put his money, however tainted it might have been, into various philanthropic projects, such as a public school and building the first Baptist church in America. John was also an early supporter of the College in the English Colony of Rhode Island and Providence Plantations, popularly known simply as Rhode Island College. John advocated mightily to have the college opened in Providence rather than in Newport. He and his allies won the hard-fought political and economic battle, and work began on the college edifice in 1770, with his financial support. When completed, it was the largest building in Rhode Island at the time, and today the college he and others championed bears the family name—Brown University. In many ways, John Brown's story is the story of Providence.

In his private life, he seems to have been a hearty bon vivant. His calling card had his information on one side, with a Jack of Spades, a one-eyed Jack, on the other. When a mob gathered to protest the performance of an itinerant theater group, John took a cannon from one of his slave ships and aimed it at the protestors until they dispersed, and the performance was allowed to go on.

John was one of the men who complained to Deputy Governor Sessions about the *Gaspee*'s depredations and the excesses of her commanding

A miniature portrait of John Brown by Newport native Edward Greene Malbone. Having a miniature Malbone portrait was something of a status symbol at the time. *Collection of the New-York Historical Society.*

officer. He was also (probably) a member of the shadowy Sons of Liberty. If anyone should know that the *Gaspee* was run aground and helpless, Lindsay must have reasoned, it was John Brown.

We don't know how or where Lindsay found him, but find him he did. It might have been at Sabin's Tavern on Town Street, today's South Main Street. Or it might have been elsewhere. Upon hearing the news, John Brown lost no time in deciding upon a course of action. While he himself never left a direct statement about that night, one participant, Ephraim Bowen, did. "Mr. Brown immediately resolved on her destruction," Bowen would recall many years later.

John Brown sent out the word to several of the men who had served as captains aboard his slave vessels and privateers, men with experience on the water, notably Abraham Whipple. They were to meet at Sabin's Tavern immediately.

Abe Whipple was one of the best sailors in the colony. In 1759, in command of the *Game Cock,* a privateer owned by the Brown brothers,

A vintage postcard portrait of Commodore Abraham Whipple, after the official Edward Savage portrait hanging at the U.S. Naval Academy. *Courtesy Providence Public Library.*

Whipple cruised the Caribbean and captured twenty-three French prizes. Some sources place the number even higher. It is no surprise that he would later be made commodore of the tiny Rhode Island navy and go on to serve with some distinction during the Revolution. On that night, he was one of a number of men who stood ready to assist John Brown in his risky venture.

According to Ephraim Bowen:

> *About the time of the shutting up of the shops, soon after sunset, a man passed along the main street, beating a drum, and informing inhabitants that the Gaspee was aground at Namquid Point, and would not float off until three o'clock the next morning; and inviting those persons who felt disposed to go and destroy that troublesome vessel to repair to Mr. James Sabin's house.*

Among the many who heard that drum was twenty-one-year-old John Mawney, variously described as a doctor or surgeon. Where he came by his medical training is uncertain. There were medical schools in New York and Philadelphia at the time, but we have nothing to suggest that he attended either of them. In any event, medicine was not a particularly advanced science in the eighteenth century, and surgeons were still often regarded as only being a step above tradesmen; in previous centuries, the nearest surgeon was the local barber. Mawney's duties would have included bleeding patients, offering them purgatives to get the humors flowing properly and setting broken bones and treating wounds in ways that are a far cry from today's highly skilled medical professionals. It is interesting to note that Mawney (an Anglicized form of the Huguenot name, Le Monie) lived at 135 Benefit Street, H.P. Lovecraft's infamous "Shunned House."

As a doctor and not a merchant, Mawney had no particular reason to care about a stranded revenue schooner. However, he had no love for the British.

On March 5, 1770, in Boston, some petty bickering between a wigmaker's apprentice and a "lobsterback"—a British soldier we today would call a redcoat—got out of hand. The argument over a supposedly unpaid bill (which had in fact been paid) escalated when the lobsterback hit the apprentice with the butt of his musket. An angry crowd soon gathered to taunt the offending soldier, and the man sent for reinforcements from a nearby barracks. By the time the officer of the watch, Captain Preston, had arrived with more men, the crowd numbered in the hundreds and pelted the lobsterbacks with snowballs and debris, daring them to fire. Innkeeper Richard Palmes knocked down a Private Montgomery, who quickly regained his feet and fired his musket into the crowd. Palmes whirled and struck Preston, and the lobsterbacks opened fire. When the smoke cleared, three men were dead, and two more would later die of their wounds.

Preston and eight of his men were arrested and tried for murder. Future president John Adams handled the defense, winning acquittal for

The site of the Boston Massacre is marked by a circle of cobblestones next to the Old Town Hall, known as the Massachusetts Town House at the time. It was sneeringly referred to as "Butcher's Hall" by colonists after the Massacre. *Photo by Judith Reilly*.

six of the soldiers. Two were found guilty of manslaughter. They escaped the death penalty and were instead branded on the thumb (this would indicate they claimed "benefit of clergy," essentially throwing themselves on the mercy of the church; the branding was done to document the fact that a man had done it once and could not claim benefit of clergy a second time). Preston was also acquitted, as he never gave the order to fire, though many of the public thought he must have.

The five deaths resulting from an argument over a wig went down in history as the Boston Massacre, one of the most frequently-cited episodes leading up to the Revolutionary War.

Two of the unfortunate victims of the massacre were John Mawney's friends. We don't know which two, but years later, Mawney wrote that Dudingston's harassment of Rhode Island colonists "added to the

A vintage postcard view of Sabin's Tavern. Originally located at the corner of today's South Main and Planet Streets, the building is long gone but is marked with a granite monument. *Courtesy Providence Public Library.*

resentment I felt for Capt. Preston ordering his company to fire on the citizens of Boston (by which, with two others) two of my intimate acquaintances and friends were killed." Dr. Mawney went along to see what all the hubbub was about as men gathered outside Sabin's Tavern.

The tavern occupied the first floor of a not-quite-finished building opposite the wharves and warehouses along the Providence waterfront. Before they had their own hall, it was the regular meeting place of the St. John's Lodge—the Providence Lodge of Freemasons—and also of the Sons of Liberty. There is some question of exactly how structured and organized the Sons of Liberty were; some sources paint them as a true secret society, while others consider "Sons of Liberty" to be a blanket term applied to pretty much anyone opposed to British authority. There was considerable overlap in membership between the Freemasons and the Sons of Liberty, and anyone belonging to one group was probably a member of the other as well. John Brown, for instance, belonged to both. (An interesting aside: many years ago, I was approached by a local Freemason who told me that he had seen the minutes book for the St. John's Lodge. He said that according to the book, there was a meeting scheduled for that night, but the entry reads, "No meeting tonight, more pressing business at hand." I have been unable to confirm the veracity of this story. If this is true, it would help explain why John Brown gathered everyone at the tavern; the major players knew where it was, and many of them may have already been heading there for the meeting.)

John Brown, "resolved on her destruction," marshaled his forces in the taproom, issuing orders. Abe Whipple reported for duty, along with Ephraim Bowen, whose family distilling business had likely been hurt by the *Gaspee*'s crackdown. Rufus Greene was there, still smarting over the loss of the *Fortune* and ready to have his vengeance. According to local tradition, the men gathered in the taproom represented a who's who of early Rhode Island history, men whose names we recognize today from the schools, streets and parks across the state named after them: Joseph

A mural that once adorned the lobby of the Providence National Bank on Westminster Street in downtown Providence, depicting the arrival of the news at Sabin's Tavern. We might wonder if the interior of the tavern was quite so grand. The bank building, sadly, was razed to make way for a condo tower that was never built. *Courtesy Henry A.L. Brown.*

Jenckes, Simeon Olney, Captain Joseph Tillinghast and others. Also on hand were a number of teenagers apprenticed to John Brown.

John laid out his plan of attack. Taking several longboats moored nearby, they would row down Narragansett Bay to Namquit Point and attack the helpless *Gaspee*. We can imagine a roar of approval echoing in the confines of the taproom at this news. In the kitchen, a few men melted down lead to cast bullets, and others, without weapons, spilled out into the street to gather up boathooks or paving stones to use.

Some friends of John Mawney's convinced him to go along. It was going to be a dangerous adventure, and they might need a doctor before the night was over. Moved in part by his lingering resentment of the British, Mawney agreed and threw his lot in with the raiders.

The front of the modern monument marking the site of Sabin's Tavern, replacing the earlier slate plaque. *Author's collection.*

The other side of the monument in the corner of the parking lot where Sabin's Tavern once stood. *Author's collection.*

Eight longboats were commandeered for the operation, and the men took time to muffle the oars, wrapping the oarlocks to prevent or minimize squeaking or scraping—sound carried well over open water, and they didn't want to be discovered sneaking up on their target.

With a smirk, John Brown declared himself the sheriff of the expedition and dubbed Abraham Whipple the captain, placing him in command of the little flotilla. About ten o'clock, they pushed off into the night, sixty or eighty men ready to have their revenge on the *Gaspee* and her hated commander.

Chapter 6

BURNED TO THE WATERLINE

The men in the longboats weren't the only ones on the water that night.

Aaron Briggs was a teenager from Portsmouth, and he is usually described as a "mulatto." Information about him is scanty, but Ezra Stiles, the amazing Newport polymath and diarist who deserves a book of his own, wrote in his diary: "This fellow's mother was an Indian at Little Compton and being born free was by the Town Council put out as a poor child in youth to a man on Prudence till aet. 24 as usual with Indian or Negro children." Stiles thought Aaron was twenty-one or older, though most others think he must have been younger, placing his age at about sixteen. He had been indentured to the family of Samuel Thurston on Prudence Island.

Indentured servants were contracted to serve until they reached a particular age (twenty-four, in Aaron's case) or sometimes until a particular date. The contract describing the terms of the agreement would be written twice on one sheet of paper and then cut in two, with each party getting a copy. The zigzag pattern used in making the cut helped prevent forgery—the halves had to match when brought back together—and also formed the basis of the term "indentured," from the uneven, toothlike edge.

Aaron was on the water that dark night to drop off a boat that Captain Thurston was lending to a friend in Bristol. At about ten o'clock, when he was some five miles from the Bristol shore, he met Simeon Potter and some other men in a boat crossing the bay, heading for Namquit Point.

Potter called out, asking who was in that boat, and when Aaron answered, Potter ordered him to come alongside. Aaron did so, probably with some trepidation. He recognized Simeon Potter, having seen him on a wharf in Bristol sometime before. If Potter in turn recognized him, he gave no indication.

Potter told Aaron that he wanted him to accompany them, saying only that they were going about a mile away but offering no specifics. Aaron refused, saying that he needed to go home. Potter insisted and Aaron again refused, saying Thurston would punish him and would flog him for being out all night.

"I can't," is all he would say to Potter.

"There is no can't in the matter," Potter called back, losing whatever patience he might have had. "You must go along with me. We shall be back in an hour." He offered Aaron two dollars to join them.

Aaron gave in and tied his little boat to Potter's. As they rowed across the bay, Potter told him that "they were going to burn the man-of-war schooner."

Aaron protested, quite reasonably, that he might lose his life in such a reckless attack. Potter grimly replied that "they were all upon their lives" and gave Aaron a handspike for a weapon. The rest were armed with cutlasses and some with muskets.

About an hour later, they rendezvoused with the other boats coming down from Providence.

A quick glance at a map, coupled with the statement Aaron would later give, shows that the attack on the *Gaspee* was more coordinated than most versions of the story indicate. Providence is north of Namquit Point. Bristol, where Potter was coming from, is to the south of the Point—and on the opposite side of the bay. Word of the planned attack must have quickly traveled from Providence to Bristol, a journey of some seventeen miles. Perhaps Potter himself carried the news. A rendezvous must have been decided upon in advance, as it seems incredibly unlikely that Potter could just happen upon the longboats coming down from Providence on the open water in the dead of night.

There is a minor oral tradition in Bristol that Potter's men disguised themselves as Indians, though there is neither testimony nor evidence to support this claim. Aaron Briggs himself makes no mention of it—and one might expect him to—and neither do any other eyewitness accounts. It is possible that this bit of oral folklore caught on after the more famous Boston Tea Party. It wouldn't be the first time a bit of history got reworked.

We aren't sure why Potter pressed Aaron into service. One theory, related to the above, maintains that Potter, trying to lend credence to the idea that his men were Indians, wanted someone with Indian blood along on the expedition. This seems a bit of a stretch. It seems easier to believe that Simeon Potter, the man who once ransacked a church and was probably still something of a pirate at heart, may have intended to plunder the *Gaspee* and simply wanted another boat along to hold the loot.

Several of the men involved left behind statements describing their version of that night's events—John Mawney, Ephraim Bowen and Aaron Briggs, along with Dudingston and a handful of his crewmen. The accounts differ in some respects—no one from the *Gaspee* makes any mention of chasing the *Hannah*, for instance; they maintain they were on their way to Providence to pick up some sailors to be transferred to another ship—but the stories agree more than they disagree, and it is possible to piece together a narrative that is probably at least fairly accurate.

At about 12:45 a.m., crewman Bartholomew Cheever was keeping the watch on the deck of the *Gaspee* when he "observed some longboats, about six or seven in number, full of men, drawing near to the schooner."

"Who comes there?" he called into the night.

No response.

Cheever alerted Dudingston, who appeared on deck in his nightshirt, with a pistol in one hand and his "hanger"—sword—in the other.

"Damn your blood, we have you now!" someone in the boats shouted.

"I came upon deck and hailed the boats," Dudingston later said, "forbidding them to come near the schooner, or I should order them fired upon."

"I am the sheriff of the County of Kent, God damn you," Abe Whipple called. "I have a warrant to apprehend you, God damn you. So surrender, God damn you!"

(According to John Mawney's account, "Captain Whipple roared out 'I am the Sheriff of the County of Kent, I am come for the commander of this vessel, and have him I will, dead or alive. Men, spring to your oars!'" Whatever his exact words were, he was not in fact the sheriff of anywhere.)

Dudingston tried to bring the *Gaspee*'s guns to bear on the approaching boats; he must have been referring to the smaller swivel-mounted guns rather than any of the eight cannon aboard. The boats approached from the north, on the *Gaspee*'s bow, perpendicular to the alignment of the cannon. But the sailors who were summoned to the deck couldn't get the guns aimed in time.

In one of the longboats, Joseph Bucklin turned to his friend Ephraim Bowen, pointing to Dudingston and saying, "Eph, reach me your gun—I can kill that fellow."

Bowen, perhaps too easily influenced by a member of his peer group, handed over his gun. It might have been a pistol or it might have been a musket; Bowen doesn't say, and historians have debated the question for years. Regardless, Joseph Bucklin fired what many consider the first shot of the Revolution, and Dudingston fell wounded to the deck.

"I have killed the rascal!" Bucklin shouted in triumph.

"Damn you, we have you!" someone else called as the boats converged on the *Gaspee* and the men swarmed aboard.

John Mawney leaped from his boat to grab at a hanging rope. He slipped and fell waist deep in the water, but a moment later, he had hauled himself aboard the schooner. Gripping the staff he had been given, he wound up to swing at one of the crewmen—apparently, the young surgeon had left "First, do no harm" somewhere behind him on a Providence wharf. Simeon Olney warned him, "John, don't strike," and instead, Mawney assisted in tying up several of the sailors.

Lieutenant Dudingston lay bleeding on the deck, wounded in the groin and the arm. According to the version of the story told by the raiders, only one shot was fired from the boats, by Joseph Bucklin. It may have been a bizarre ricochet, with the musket ball entering the arm and bouncing to the groin. But according to some of the *Gaspee* men, they managed to fire off a volley of small-arms fire before the raiders got aboard, raising the possibility that one of those shots went wide and Dudingston was also wounded by one of his own men.

A few of the men, no doubt friends of Rufus Greene's, demanded to know if the lieutenant planned to make amends for the seizure of the *Fortune* and its cargo. Someone, probably not Rufus himself, suggested that they would turn the *Gaspee* back over to her commander if he agreed.

But Dudingston began to drag himself aft, toward his cabin.

"Now you piratical rascal, we have got you," someone cried. "Damn you, we will hang you by all the laws of Great Britain. Damn you, what made you fire when we answered you that the head sheriff was in the boat?"

Another nineteenth-century depiction of the attack. *Courtesy the Rhode Island Historical Society. Engraving by J. Rogers after a painting by J. McNevin. The Burning of the Gaspee. RI 1856. Ink on paper. RHi X3 119.*

"Lord have mercy upon me," Dudingston begged. "I am done for."

Suddenly, the giant figure of John Brown loomed above him, silhouetted against the nighttime sky and wielding a handspike.

"Stand aside," he commanded. "Let me dispatch this piratical dog!"

Dudingston protested that he was already mortally wounded.

"Damn your blood—you are shot by your own people," John Brown snapped.

Dudingston was in no position to argue the point just then. Realizing that he and his men were outnumbered probably three or four to one, he ordered the *Gaspee*'s surrender. John Brown slowly lowered the spike and told his men to carry Dudingston to his cabin. He then called for John Mawney, saying he was wanted immediately.

"What is the matter, Mr. Brown?" the young surgeon asked.

"Don't call names," John Brown warned. "But go immediately into the cabin. There is one wounded and will bleed to death."

Several men crowded into the lieutenant's small cabin. When Mawney entered within a few minutes, John Brown and Abe Whipple pushed their way in and began to go through the papers on the bureau, demanding to see Dudingston's orders. When he pointed them out, Brown and Whipple pocketed the papers, saying they would scrutinize them later at their leisure.

Mawney examined his patient. Dudingston had wrapped a blanket around himself, and pulling it aside, Mawney "discovered the effect of a musket ball in his left groin." Dudingston was in serious danger, hemorrhaging profusely from the wound. The bleeding needed to be stopped, and having no bandages, the young doctor pulled off his vest and began tearing strips from his shirt.

"Pray, sir, don't tear your clothes," Dudingston said. "There is linen in that trunk."

Mawney ordered Joseph Bucklin, the same man who had shot Dudingston in the first place, to break open the trunk and tear him some bandages. He also told Bucklin to scrape lint from the linen—this may have been meant to pack the wound—but the linen was too new and strong, and Bucklin couldn't produce any lint. Despite this, Mawney did manage to extract at least part of the ball, prepare bandages and compresses and, wrapping the wound tightly, stop the bleeding. He may very well have saved the lieutenant's life.

Perhaps remembering that he was supposed to be an officer and a gentleman, even when he had been shot in the groin, Dudingston offered his surgeon a token of gratitude: a gold stock buckle. A stock buckle secured a gentleman's fine formal neckwear, his stock, and while worn at the back of the neck they could be quite ornate and decorated with gemstones. Mawney declined the offer—perhaps the design was too military for his taste—but he did accept a silver one that Dudingston offered next. It would be ungentlemanly to refuse a second time.

Dawn was breaking, lighting the eastern sky. It was time to go. John Brown ordered the raiders to place the bound sailors into the longboats and prepare to row them ashore. He gave strict orders that no one was to remove anything from the *Gaspee*. There must be nothing that could connect any of them to the attack.

Dudingston was carried out of his cabin in his blanket and placed in a boat with Aaron Briggs and the expedition's captain, Abraham Whipple. As they rowed away from the schooner, Whipple told Dudingston that if he did not agree to pay for the rum he had seized when he captured the *Fortune*, he should not expect anything belonging to him saved— presumably up to and including the *Gaspee* herself. Dudingston replied that he would pay whatever the law required and the raiders could do as they pleased.

They rowed ashore at Pawtuxet's Stillhouse Cove, a short distance away. Five of Dudingston's men were untied to carry him onto the beach.

Back aboard the *Gaspee*, John Brown stood alone on the deck. He made sure everyone else had disembarked, and disembarked empty-handed, before he was ready to leave himself.

We don't know who put the *Gaspee* to the torch. None of the men who later made statements admitted to doing it. It is possible that it could have been John Brown himself, but it also could have been Abe Whipple, Simeon Potter or perhaps even a vengeful Rufus Greene. We may never know. But whoever it was, the *Gaspee* was in flames before John Brown stepped into the safety of the last longboat. The powder kegs in the magazine were said to have exploded, though none of the contemporary accounts mentions this. Regardless, the flames must have lit the sky and been visible from the cove where Dudingston lay, as his first command went up in smoke.

John Brown only ever spoke of his involvement in the attack once. As an old man, he told his grandson, future governor John Brown Francis, about it. "Mr. Brown was the last man to leave the deck, being determined that no one should carry from the vessel anything which might lead to the identification and detection of the parties," Mr. Francis recalled. "By doing so, he narrowly escaped with his life, in consequence of the falling timbers and spars."

Onshore, Dudingston and his men were brought to nearby houses. The crewmen were locked in the cellar of a house on Peck Lane and held

A plaque at Stillhouse Cove, near today's Rhode Island Yacht Club, marks the picturesque spot where the wounded Dudingston was brought ashore. *Author's collection.*

Close-up of the plaque. *Author's collection.*

there overnight. The house is long gone, but a plaque marks the spot. Dudingston was carried to the house of Joseph Rhodes, a local Tory, a short distance away.

On the waters of the bay, the raiders disbanded. Simeon Potter dismissed Aaron Briggs and sent him on his way. We don't know if he came across with the two dollars he had promised. The men rowed back to their homes, leaving the smoldering wreck of the *Gaspee* far behind them; she is usually described as being burned to the waterline.

This was more serious than burning a stolen boat in the center of town, and even more serious than taking a few potshots at the retreating *St. John.* These men had wounded a British officer and destroyed one of His Majesty's vessels. This was sedition. This was treason. Simeon Potter was right; they were all upon their lives. If they were caught, they would hang.

Every one of them.

Chapter 7

KEEPING UP
APPEARANCES

Word of the night's event spread quickly as the sun rose over Providence. Anyone who hadn't heard the news over breakfast certainly knew by lunchtime.

Abe Whipple had disobeyed John Brown's stern wishes and made off with a silver goblet, perhaps from Dudingston's own room. After being handed down through Whipple's descendants for some generations, it is today in the collection of the Rhode Island Historical Society. At some point in its history, the family engraved the cup, noting its significance but getting the date wrong, inscribing it with June 17, 1772.

Another article that somehow made its way off the ship that night was, surprisingly, Dudingston's hat, which fell into the hands of a young boy. According to William Staples, an early historian of the event:

> *Mr. John Howland says that on the morning after the affair Justin Jacobs, a young man, was parading himself on "the great bridge," then the usual place of resort, with Lieutenant Duddingston's gold laced beaver on his head, detailing to a circle around him the particulars of the transaction and the manner in which he obtained the hat from the*

The wine goblet Abe Whipple stole from the *Gaspee* that fateful night. *Courtesy the Rhode Island Historical Society. Gaspee Wine Goblet. England. 1770. Silver. RHi X31938.*

cabin of the Gaspee. *It required sharp words to induce him to retire and hold his peace.*

When the news reached him, Deputy Governor Darius Sessions immediately swung into action. Remembering the complaint lodged with him about Dudingston's conduct back in March, he knew who the lieutenant's critics were and probably realized that many, if not most, of those who had signed that complaint must have been involved in the attack. And this was no mere episode of drunken mischief by some ne'er-do-wells. This was serious business. The Crown threatened to revoke charters for less. He needed to at least appear to be concerned, even if he kept his real concerns well hidden.

Sessions rode out to Pawtuxet to check on Dudingston, finding him languishing at Joseph Rhodes's house. Sessions "told him if he needed money, surgeons, or a removal of his person to a place more convenient, I would give him all the assistance in my power."

Dudingston said he wanted no such favors for himself, but he requested that his men be sent to safety, either being conveyed to Admiral Montagu in Boston or sent over to the *Beaver*, anchored in Newport. Sessions promised to see what he could do.

Sessions then asked Dudingston to make a formal statement giving his version of the attack, but "he would give me no account of the matter; first, because of his indisposition of body, and secondly, because it was his duty to forbear any thing of the nature till he had done it to his

The marker on Peck Lane, in Pawtuxet, near the site where the *Gaspee* prisoners were briefly held in a cellar. *Author's collection.*

Close-up of the plaque designed by local artist Chris Kane. *Author's collection.*

commanding officer, at a court martial, to which, if he lived, he must be called, but if he died, he desired it might all die with him."

Dudingston was probably being a bit melodramatic here. Sessions asked his permission to interview the sailors. Dudingston consented, and Sessions took affidavits from Bartholomew Cheever, the man who had been on watch when the raiders approached, and two others: boatswain John Johnson and seaman William J. Caple. Sessions or an assistant took down the statements, and the three illiterate sailors signed with Xs.

All the statements told the same basic story—they were on their way to Providence to pick up some sailors and transfer them to another ship when they had run aground and been attacked in the dead of night. Their commander had been shot, and they were rowed ashore and left in Pawtuxet by their attackers. Sessions asked each man if he recognized any of the raiders and must have breathed a sigh of relief when each of them answered no, it had been too dark.

The deputy governor then returned to Providence and sent the affidavits he had obtained to Governor Wanton, along with a summary of his conversation with Dudingston.

"The dangerous tendency of this transaction it too obvious, to pass over with the least appearance of neglect," Sessions observed in his letter to the governor, "and therefore, doubt not that Your Honor will give it due attention, and prosecute such matters as wisdom and prudence shall dictate.

"It is the prevailing opinion of the gentlemen in this quarter," he went on, "that a proclamation, with a large reward, be issued, for apprehending the persons who have thus offended."

He dispatched the letter to Wanton in Newport and sat back to look over the day's work. He had acted quickly and decisively, expressing concern for the wounded Dudingston and disapproval for the "very disagreeable affair." He had alerted the governor and advised him to offer a reward for the capture of the perpetrators. Clearly, he had done all that was within his power. He had kept up appearances.

And he had also discovered that those perpetrators had all gone unrecognized by the *Gaspee*'s crew. It was a minor miracle. Sessions hadn't been in one of the longboats himself that night, but his sympathies certainly were. If he could pull a few strings, they might all actually get away with it.

That same morning, Dudingston sent midshipman William Dickinson to report the *Gaspee*'s loss to Admiral Montagu in Boston. Montagu questioned Dickinson, an eyewitness to the attack, taking down the man's statement and sending a copy to the British official Wills Hill, Lord Hillsborough and secretary of state for the colonies. Lord Hillsborough had the kind of impatience with colonists only a British bureaucrat could have.

Montagu informed Hillborough that "the lawless and piratical people of Rhode Island obliges me to write to you." The bold actions of this "nest of daring smugglers" compelled him to ask for "Your Lordship's instructions for what is to be done."

Before the ink was even dry on that letter, he fired off another one to Governor Wanton. He could not have been looking forward to renewing their correspondence. He included another copy of Dickinson's deposition and condemned "the piratical proceedings of the people of Providence…by attacking His Majesty's schooner with an armed force." He urged Wanton to "use such methods as you shall think proper for apprehending and bringing the offenders to justice." He coolly informed Wanton that he had apprised his superiors in the British government of the situation.

Wanton had to admit that this was serious.

As if losing his first command and getting shot in the crotch wasn't bad enough, insult was soon piled upon injury when the sheriff—the real sheriff—arrived to serve Dudingston with papers. The Greene family was suing him for seizing the *Fortune* and sending her to Boston.

The crew of the *Gaspee* were handed over to Captain Linzee aboard the *Beaver*, a fourteen-gun sloop of war in Newport Harbor. Sessions arranged the transportation and afterward promptly submitted a bill to the General Assembly for nine pounds and one shilling to cover the cost of his trip to Pawtuxet and for getting the Royal Navy men back to Newport.

Sessions wrote to Wanton again a couple of days later, once again urging him to "issue a proclamation, with proper reward, for the apprehending and bringing to justice any and every person that was concerned in destroying the schooner *Gaspee*, or in assaulting and wounding William Dudingston, the commander of said schooner."

Sessions's latest letter included the somewhat snide observation that "some exceptions are taken at the *Gaspee*'s being called His Majesty's schooner, as it is thought by some, she, in fact, really was not, and consequently did not deserve that appellation. If the evidence we have in that respect be sufficient to denominate her as a King's vessel, she ought to be called so; if not, then only without compliment, the schooner *Gaspee*."

In a postscript, Sessions told the governor that "Dr. Sterling, who attends Capt. Dudingston, informed us yesterday that he is in a fair way to recover from his wounds."

The courier who delivered Sessions's letter to Wanton in Newport probably brought back the proclamation, dated the same day, June 12, 1772:

By the Honorable Joseph Wanton, Esquire, Governor, Captain General and Commander-in-chief of and over the English Colony of Rhode Island and Providence Plantations in New England in America—

A Proclamation.

Whereas, on Tuesday, the 9th inst., in the night, a number of people unknown, boarded his Majesty's armed schooner the Gaspee, *as she lay aground on a point of land called Namquit, a little to the southward of Pawtuxet, in the colony aforesaid, who dangerously wounded William Dudingston, the commander, and by force took him with all his people, put them into boats, and landed them near Pawtuxet, and afterward set fire to the said schooner, whereby she was totally destroyed.*

I have, therefore, thought fit, by and with the advice of such of his Majesty's council as could be seasonably convened to issue this proclamation, strictly charging and commanding all his majesty's officers within the said colony, both civil and military, to exert themselves with the utmost vigilance to discover and apprehend the persons guilty of the aforesaid atrocious crime, that they may be brought to condign punishment, and I do hereby offer a reward of ONE HUNDRED POUNDS, *Sterling money of Great Britain to any person or persons who shall discover the perpetrators of the said villainy, to be paid immediately upon the conviction of any one or more of them.*

And the several sheriffs in the said colony are hereby required forthwith to cause this proclamation to be posted up in the most public places in each of the towns in their respective countries.

Given under my hand and seal at arms at Newport this 12th day of June, in the twelfth year of the reign of his Most Sacred Majesty George the Third, by the Grace of God, King of Great Britain and so forth, Anno Dom. 1772.

J. Wanton.

By his Honor's command:
Henry Ward, Secretary.
God Save the King.

By *the Honorable* JOSEPH WANTON, *Esquire, Governor,*
Captain General, and Commander in Chief, of and over the Englifh
(L. S.) *Colony of* Rhode-Ifland, *and* Providence Plantations, *in* New-England,
in America.

A   PROCLAMATION.

HEREAS on *Tuefday*, the ninth Inftant in the Night, a Number of People, unknown, boarded His Majefty's armed Schooner
the *Gafpee*, as fhe lay aground on a Point of Land, called
Nanquit, a little to the fouthward of *Pawtuxet*, in the Colony
aforefaid, who dangeroufly wounded Lieutenant *William Dud-*
ingfton the Commander, and by Force took him with all his
People, put them into Boats, and landed them near *Paw-*
tuxet ; and afterwards fet Fire to the faid Schooner, whereby fhe was entirely de-
ftroyed :

I HAVE, therefore, thought fit, by and with the Advice of fuch of His Majefty's Council, as could be feafonably convened, to iffue this Proclamation, ftrict-
ly charging and commanding all His Majefty's Officers within the faid Colony, both Civil and Military, to exert themfelves with the utmoft Vigilance, to difcover and apprehend the Perfons guilty of the aforefaid atrocious Crime, that
they may be brought to condign Punifhment. And I do hereby offer a Reward
of ONE HUNDRED POUNDS, Sterling Money of *Great-*
Britain, to any Perfon or Perfons who fhall difcover the Perpetrators of the
faid Villainy, to be paid immediately upon the Conviction of any one or more
of them.

AND the feveral Sheriffs in the faid Colony are hereby required, forthwith, to
caufe this Proclamation to be pofted up in the moft public Places, in each of the
Towns in their refpective Counties.

GIVEN under my Hand and Seal at Arms, at Newport, *this Twelfth Day of*
June, in the Twelfth Year of the Reign of His Moft Sacred Majefty, GEORGE
THE THIRD, *by the Grace of God, King of* Great-Britain, *and fo forth,*
Annoq; Dom. One Thoufand, Seven Hundred and Seventy-two.

J. WANTON.

By his Honor's Command,
HENRY WARD, *Sec'ry.*

GOD   SAVE   THE   KING.

Governor Wanton's proclamation describing the burning of the *Gaspee* and offering £100
for "the perpetrators of the said villainy." *Courtesy the Rhode Island Historical Society. Joseph*
Wanton. A Proclamation. RI. 1772. Ink on Paper. RHi X17 563.

The story was reported in the *Providence Gazette*'s edition for June 13. The brief article covered the basics of the story, adding:

> *We hear that one Dagget, belonging to the Vineyard, who had served the before mentioned schooner as a pilot, but at the time of her being destroyed was on board the* Beaver *sloop of war, going ashore a few days since at Narragansett to a sheep-shearing, was seized by the company, who cut off his hair, and performed on him the operation of shearing in such a manner that his ears and nose were in imminent danger.*

Between the newspapers and copies of the proclamation being hung up in "the most public places," not to mention the rampant gossip going around, everyone in the colony knew what had happened. Many, if not most, knew the names of the men responsible.

Darius Sessions, John Brown and the rest just had to make sure everyone kept their mouths shut.

Chapter 8

LOOSE LIPS

There were, of course, some loyal Tories left in Rhode Island who must have been shocked at the attack. With the punishment meted out to Loyalists during the Stamp Act crisis a few years before, they had learned to keep a low profile, understanding they were in the minority; none of them wanted to get tarred and feathered or hanged in effigy. One of them, we don't know who, turned informant and sent Montagu a report detailing the rumors that had been making their way around Providence.

According to the report, Dudingston's crackdown on smuggling made him "very troublesome to the trading vessels that wished to go on in the old way. His vigilance alarmed the gentlemen in trade at Providence so much that they in a memorial to our governor represented Duddingston as a pirate." The informant reports that Dudingston had long been a target, as "great pains were taken to decoy him ashore, and when that failed they threatened to serve his Schooner in the same way that they had done the…Sloop *Liberty*."

The unknown informant maintains that the *Gaspee* running aground was no accident but a deliberate act on Lindsay's part:

> *One of the Providence packets, being a good sailor, disregarded the signal*
> *& refused to be brought to by Captain Duddingston, who immediately*

weighed and followed him up the river. The master of the packet knowing the river well, run into shallow water, where he knew if Capt. Duddingston followed him with the schooner he must get ashore—this happened agreeable to his expectations…

…As soon as the master of the packet got up to the town he gave the alarm, on which a party beat up through the town of Providence for volunteers, and in the night about eleven o'clock, fifty or sixty men, armed, whose faces and hands were all blacked, embarked in six or seven boats, got very near the schooner unperceived…The two men that were the watch upon deck informed the captain that a number of boats were standing towards them very near. On this Duddingston with his two pistols in his hands, jumped up upon deck, went forward and hailed them. They answered they wanted him and by God they would have him dead or alive. He ordered them to keep off on their peril.

The informant reported more gunplay than others had: "They continued to advance and he fired his pistols amongst them, which hurt nobody. They returned the fire immediately, shot the captain in the arm, and wounded him in the body, of which it's thought he will die."

After rowing the crew ashore, the raiders "then returned again to the Schooner, hoisted in Capt. Duddingston's barge upon deck, hoisted up the sails of the King's schooner, and set her on fire, where she burnt up. Thus ended the rebellion. What will follow is yet uncertain."

Expressing contempt for the local government, the anonymous informant condemns Wanton, attempts to paint local Loyalists as victims and even proves that he is out of step with the majority of Rhode Islanders by criticizing the revered charter:

Our Governor's Proclamation, who must study to keep appearances, but if it is left to this Government to find out the Perpetrators they will I am confident remain very safe. I will not comment upon this extraordinary action. You know us well, and the many outrages we have been guilty of. Therefore I need say no more on this head; but I hope government will

> *make a proper use of this unheard of event, and take this opportunity*
> *of depriving us of what to some of us is the greatest curse, the Charter.*

The anonymous author's biggest hope was Governor Wanton's deepest fear.

Whoever he was, the informant was not alone. Another (likewise unnamed) Tory in Boston wrote to a friend in Newport that Admiral Montagu

> *is determined to lay your town, and Providence, in ashes: he swore by*
> *God (some time ago), that he would burn the town of Providence to*
> *ashes. Mr P---, of this town, will attest to it; hope you will try him*
> *for treason.*
>
> *It is surmised that they are going to deprive you of your charter; hope*
> *you will give it up peaceably like true* friend *to government, and not*
> *contend with your superiors, but be subject to the higher powers; for the*
> *powers that be are ordained, I believe, of the devil.*

A few weeks later, Aaron Briggs slipped off the Thurston family farm on Prudence Island and rowed out to the *Beaver*, the same sloop of war that had received the *Gaspee* refugees a short time before. He had been indentured to the Thurston family for as long as he could remember; the indenture was to end at age twenty-four, but for Aaron, who wasn't even certain how old he was, that may have seemed like an eternity away. Farm work was long and backbreaking, and he had to share a bed with two other indentured servants. It was hardly an easy life, and perhaps the rising tensions over the whole *Gaspee* episode proved too much and Aaron simply wanted out.

It seems unlikely that he knew just how bad his choice had been. He probably didn't know where the *Gaspee* sailors had ended up, and he couldn't know that the *Beaver*'s captain, John Linzee, would turn a deaf ear on his request for shelter. If the lad were unhappy in his situation, Linzee must have reasoned, let him go clutter up someone else's ship. No need to involve the *Beaver*. He condemned Aaron as a runaway and had him put in irons. He'd flog the mulatto in the morning and teach him to waste the Royal Navy's time before sending him on his way.

The next day, Aaron Briggs was tied to a mast, and the crew gathered to watch. Floggings were entertainment. As the cat-o'-nine-tails was readied, one of the *Gaspee*'s men jumped up, saying that he recognized Aaron. The man, Patrick Earle, told Linzee that the teenager tied to the mast had been one of the raiders who attacked the *Gaspee*. Linzee took them both aside and asked Earle if he was certain. He was.

As the *Gaspee* burned, Earle had been shoved into one of the longboats along with Lieutenant Dudingston—the longboat with Aaron Briggs at one of the oars. Aaron had, in fact, untied Earle to have him help with the rowing. It was him, Earle insisted, he could swear to it. And Linzee did have Earle swear on the ship's Bible.

The captain then turned to Aaron and said, "My lad, you see this man has declared you was there, and if you don't tell me who was there with you, I will hang you at the yard arm immediately. And if you do, you shall not be hurt."

Aaron Briggs almost certainly did not go aboard the *Beaver* intending to name names. But now, he had been called out and threatened with execution if he did not. He had no loyalty to the men who attacked the schooner; Simeon Potter had dragged him into the whole mess.

Aaron gave a brief description of the raid upon the *Gaspee* and named John Brown and Simeon Potter as the ringleaders, along with a "Doctor Weeks, of Warwick," and someone named Richmond, supposedly from Providence.

Linzee dispatched a report to Montagu, and Montagu in turn wrote a triumphant letter to Governor Wanton.

Boston, 8th July, 1772.
Sir:—By express last night from Capt. Linzee, of his Majesty's sloop Beaver, *I received the enclosed account; and, although it comes from a negro man, it carries with it the appearance of truth, as it agrees in many circumstances with Lieutenant Dudingston's letter, (to me,) and also with the deposition of the midshipman of the* Gaspee; *add to this, a man belonging*

to the Gaspee, *swears to this negro's being in the boat that put him ashore, and challenged him as soon as he saw him on board the* Beaver.

These corroborating circumstances put it out of all doubt with me that he was actually concerned in taking and burning the King's schooner. And as he has impeached several others that were concerned in that piratical act, I am to beg your Excellency, will get the people mentioned in the enclosed account apprehended, that they may be examined before you, in the presence of Lieutenant Dudingston, who, I dare say, will remember the person of the surgeon that dressed his wounds, and may possibly recollect the persons of Potter and Brown, who appear to me to have been the ringleaders in destroying his Majesty's schooner.

As this affair was transacted in your Excellency's government, I must totally rely on you to have these people secured and (if there is sufficient proof against them) brought to justice. I doubt not but that you will exert yourself as much as in your power, and I flatter myself, that, with your assistance, the King will have justice done him, and the offenders brought to punishment, which I hope will in future prevent the King's officers from being upon all occasions insulted, and check the lawless and piratical behavior of the people of Rhode Island.

I am, sir, your Excellency's most obedient servant,
J. MONTAGU.

In a postscript, Montagu requested that Wanton "use every proper method to get them apprehended, that they may be tried," and asked that should the governor have "a proper person" take a statement from Aaron, "that you will favor me with a copy of it."

The document included with the letter, entitled "Statement of the Negro Aaron," contained some minor errors but was still extremely damning. According to Aaron, it had been John Brown himself who fired the shot that wounded Dudingston. We know that Aaron had previously met Simeon Potter and recognized him that night, but as far as we know, the rest of the raiders were all strangers to him. In the noise, confusion and darkness, it seems likely that Aaron simply misidentified Joseph Bucklin, the man to whom Ephraim Bowen handed his gun.

His statement also names a Joseph Brown. John did have a brother named Joseph, but there has always been some question of whether he was present that night. He could have been, or Aaron could have been thinking of another Joseph, possibly even Joseph Bucklin himself. Or perhaps he remembered the name Joseph and Captain Linzee, familiar with the leading men of the colony, helpfully suggested the last name of Brown.

No one named Weeks or Richmond was specifically known to be involved in the raid. "Dr. Weeks" is clearly meant to be John Mawney, but where Aaron came up with the name Weeks is anybody's guess.

Still, aside from these fairly minor mistakes, this was a dangerous document. It was the kind of document that got men hanged.

While Joseph Wanton considered himself a loyal British subject, he agreed with so many others that the Crown was beginning to overstep its authority. Loyal opposition is a difficult position. He was extremely reluctant to hand over anyone involved, but Aaron's information placed him in an uncomfortable position.

As the governor of the colony, he had previously informed Montagu "that I do not receive instructions for the administration of my government, from the King's admiral stationed in America." He would handle the situation as he saw fit. He had no intention of handing over the men some runaway Negro teenager had fingered. He would take a different tack entirely.

He would discredit Aaron Briggs.

Wanton lost no time in contacting Samuel Thurston and obtaining statements from various members of the household regarding Aaron's whereabouts on the night the *Gaspee* was attacked.

The lad could not have had anything to do with it, Samuel Thurston insisted, being "fully persuaded the said Aaron hath not been off from the said island for more than twelve months," further adding that he thought "it absolutely impossible that the said Aaron should have been that night any where near the place where the said schooner was burnt, and that the said Aaron remained at home from the said 9th of June until the 2nd day of July, and never during that time gave him the least information suggestion or hint of his having any knowledge of the business of the schooner."

And even if Aaron had wanted to sneak off the island, Thurston said, it would have been impossible. There was only one boat available, but it was "then so much out of repair that…she could not swim, and then lay bottom upwards in order to be refitted." The boat was refitted shortly after the attack, and Aaron stole it to row himself out to the *Beaver*.

Thurston's son-in-law, Samuel Tompkins, was the man to whom Aaron was actually indentured, and he corroborated the older man's story. Some parts of their respective statements are identical, reading word for word. Clearly, they had taken the time to get their stories straight.

Somerset and Jack, the family's two other indentured servants, likewise stated that Aaron had been with them on the night in question and that they never had "the least hint or information about the attack." Somerset, "a mulatto," and Jack, "a negro," signed their joint statement with their marks.

Back aboard the *Beaver*, Captain Linzee took steps of his own. Patrick Earle, whom Aaron, for some reason, called "Paddy Alis," likewise gave a formal statement:

> *That after a number of boats boarded the said schooner as she lay aground and the people's hands were tied he with several others was put into the same boat that the captain was carried ashore in; and that he helped a negro man, called Aaron Briggs, to row the bow oar, which negro is now on board His Majesty's ship,* Beaver, *who hath sworn that he did row ashore with the bow oar, and further saith not.*

He signed his deposition with an X.

Montagu informed Dudingston where matters stood. The admiral's letter has not survived, but the lieutenant's reply has. In it, he pleads that he is "hardly able to give answer, from the painful situation I am in; nor is it possible, at present, for me to be of the least use in respect to the negro." Though he went on to say, "I have no doubt of his being in the boat with me."

Remembering the violence of the nighttime raid and the anger burning in the eyes of the men swarming aboard, Dudingston must have shuddered as he read over the names obtained from Aaron Briggs.

"I cannot help telling you, that, without I was able to retire to a ship, I should not exist one night on shore, if I was able to make oath to any of the people mentioned." He must have feared that the men would come for him again, and this time they'd finish the job. Indeed, there were rumors of armed gangs searching for him before he was moved aboard a British ship.

For Wanton, the next step was to get Aaron Briggs handed over. He wrote to Linzee:

> *As it is highly necessary that this lad should be examined by the civil authority concerning what he knows of that affair I have directed the sheriff to wait upon you and request that you would deliver Aaron into his custody, in order to be brought on shore, that such proceedings may be had and done in this matter, as are agreeably to law.*
>
> *The King's attorney general will attend the examination; and I should be glad if you, or any of your officers, would likewise attend. If you are of opinion that it is most for His Majesty's service to return Aaron on board your ship after he has been examined, instead of committing him to jail, you may be assured it shall be done.*

On July 17, two men, Sheriff Robert Lillibridge Jr. and James Brenton, found Linzee ashore and served him with the warrant for the arrest of Aaron Briggs. Or at least Brenton did—Linzee wouldn't come out of the house where they found him to face Lillibridge. He was fearful of arrest on various charges that had been filed against him and still hung over his head. Brenton, taking the lead, went over the warrant, explaining the impropriety of keeping Aaron aboard the *Beaver* when he was charged with a capital crime and wanted by the civil authorities.

Linzee snapped that he knew of no civil authority in the colony and called Governor Wanton "a damned rascal." Montagu's was the only authority he would recognize. As for the warrant, "he did not regard it any more than if it was a piece of blank paper."

Lillibridge and Brenton left empty-handed.

Wanton immediately appealed to Montagu, insisting, "I have pursued every measure in my power to investigate and find out the truth" and that "from the general bad character of the declarant [Aaron], I was fully convinced that no regard could be had to this information." Still, "it was absolutely necessary that this declarant should be delivered up to the civil authority to be properly examined." But his request was "treated by Capt. Linzee with great contempt, and by him utterly disregarded. What could be his motives or reasons for such his conduct I am not able to account for. It certainly is a great contempt of the civil authority of this colony who have the only power and jurisdiction to try all and every offence committed."

In an attempt to have Aaron released, the family had Linzee arrested.

At this point, Montagu gave up. It had become a farce. He informed Wanton of his intention to refer the whole matter to his superiors:

> *It is not in my power to do more than I have, to bring the offenders to justice. The whole must rest with you who are upon the spot. I find the master of Aaron, the black, has arrested Capt Linzee, for the detention of his servant; therefore, as Capt Linzee has done nothing but by my orders, I have bailed him, and will keep the fellow. I did intend sending him to you, had not his master taken this step.*
>
> *I shall not trouble Your Excellency any more on the subject of the* Gaspee *but leave the result of the whole conduct of His Majesty's good subjects at Rhode Island to him and his ministers and am, sir,*
> *Your most obedient humble servant*
> *J. MONTAGU*

Aaron wasn't going anywhere. Stalemate.

If he had been released back to the family, we can only guess what might have happened to him from there. He might have been sent into hiding, whisked away somewhere safe. Or he might have been punished, flogged to within an inch of his life, until he recanted his story.

It looked, at least for the moment, as though the whole thing might blow over. They had forced things to an impasse; Aaron Briggs was discredited, and John Brown could not be found—not that Wanton or his people were searching for him all that diligently. If they had been, they would have found him going about his usual business in Providence and Newport, though perhaps a bit more carefully than usual. Montagu seemed to be giving up the fight. And everyone else had kept their mouths shut.

But this was still treason, still a hanging offense. Authorities in England were not going to give up so easily.

Chapter 9

DAMAGES

O n the third Monday in July, William Dudingston, who had spent
time safely aboard ship, came ashore to face the Greenes in a court
of law. Appearing at the Kent County Courthouse in East Greenwich
and represented by Newport attorney James Brenton, he pled not guilty.

He must have known this was an utter waste of time. Seizing the
Fortune, property of a prosperous and well-connected local family, and
then knowingly overstepping his authority by sending her to Boston for
trial doomed him to failure in a Rhode Island court. He promptly lost the
case and was ordered to pay the Greene family "two hundred and ninety
five pounds lawful money for the damages they have sustained…and one
pound eighteen shillings and two pence, like money, for the cost in and
about the prosecution of this suit expended."

Dudingston and his lawyer would file two appeals and, of course, lose
them both. He was forced to pay, even though the amount would actually
be covered by Newport customs officials—the same officials the Greenes
had been dodging in the first place.

October found Dudingston back in England to face a court-martial,
as "it was incumbent upon him to account to the court for the loss of
his Majesty's schooner, the *Gaspee*, under his command." The court
before which Dudingston now appeared consisted of eight captains

A vintage postcard view of the Kent County Courthouse, where Dudingston lost his case to the Greene family. *Courtesy Shelia Quinn.*

and was convened aboard the *Centaur*, a seventy-four-gun third-rate ship of the line anchored at Portsmouth, on the south coast of England. Alongside the wounded lieutenant were five of his crewmen and Captain Linzee.

The sailors gave their accounts of the attack, and the court posed its central question to midshipman William Dickinson (who had made a statement to Darius Sessions the morning after the raid): "Do you apprehend every measure was pursued that could be on so short a notice for the preservation of His Majesty's schooner?"

To which Dickinson simply replied, "Yes."

Dudingston was allowed to pose a question of his own to Captain Linzee.

"You know the spot where the *Gaspee* was destroyed…could you suppose I could possibly have the least reason to apprehend an attack from the shore in the manner I did, being so far from the shore?"

"I am of the opinion there was no reason to apprehend any attack," Linzee affirmed, "as she lay four miles from any principal town."

Dudingston and his men backed one another up—he had no objection as to the conduct of the men serving under him, and they in turn swore that their lieutenant "did his utmost" to prevent the loss of the vessel.

The court rendered its verdict: "The court agreed that the schooner was seized in the night by a number of men in boats, and Mr. Dudingston and the rest of the officers and people belonging to her did their duty in opposing the seizure to the utmost of their power on so short a notice and they should be honorably acquitted."

The lieutenant must have breathed a sigh of relief. Justice in the British Royal Navy was absolutely draconian. Cowardice, failure to fight and allowing a ship to go aground or be wrecked—any or all of which he could conceivably have been charged with—were all offenses under the Articles of War, and all were punishable by death.

Dudingston went on to petition the Crown for relief, citing the "dangerous wounds" he had received in the line of duty.

To the King's most excellent Majesty

The Petition of Captain William Dudingston late Commander of
Your Majesty's Schooner the Gaspee
Most humbly sheweth
That your Majesty's Petitioner was ordered by Admiral Montague to
cruise in your Majesty's Schooner the Gaspee *on the Coasts of Your*
Majesty's Province of Rhode Island.
 That in the performance of his Duty on that Station he made several
Seizures, and put almost an entire Stop to the illicit Trade of that Colony;
which so exasperated the Inhabitants that at midnight between the 9th

& 10th of June 1772, while your Majesty's Schooner the Gaspee *lay aground on a Spit of Sand in Providence River several Miles from any Town, about Two hundred Men in seventeen armed long Boats attacked your Majesty's said Schooner, and after your Majesty's Petitioner was disabled from acting took & burnt Her.*

That your Majesty's Petitioner in doing his Duty in Defence of Your Majesty's said Schooner received two Musket Shot. One Ball broke & shattered his left Arm and the other lodged in the lower part of his Body.

That your Majesty's Petitioner suffered the most excruciating Pains from his Wounds for want of Proper assistance, and remained nine Weeks in a miserable Situation among the Author of his Misfortune, who daily threatened to take away his Life; until he was rescued at last by Capt. Linzee in Your Majesty's Sloop Beaver *with an armed force.*

That Your Majesty's Petitioner still labors under a painful, expensive and hitherto ineffectual Cure, having a Ball lodged in the lower part of his Body which cannot be extracted, and not having the Use of his left Arm; so that Pains & Lameness are probably entailed on him for Life.

That what little Property Your Majesty's Petitioner had was with him in Your Majesty's said Schooner with Her was burnt & destroyed.

That Your Majesty's Petitioner has been tried by a Court Martial for the loss of Your Majesty's said Schooner and honorably acquitted.

Your Majesty's Petitioner therefore most humbly prays that Your Majesty would be graciously pleased to take his Case into Your Royal Consideration and grant him such Support as in Your Majesty's Wisdom shall seem fit. And Your Majesty's Petitioner as in Duty bound shall ever pray &c, &c, &c.

W. Dudingston

Dudingston seems to be giving in to his penchant for melodrama here and patting himself on the back at the same time. It is seriously doubtful that he "put almost an entire Stop to the illicit Trade of that Colony." He also exaggerated the number of raiders, as most historians put the number at sixty or eighty. But Dudingston makes it sound as if he stood single-handed against an army. Still, he was awarded a pension of ninety-one pounds, five shillings and was later rumored to be convalescing at a French spa.

Admiral Montagu had dispatched several reports to officials in England enclosing the various statements and affidavits. It would be weeks before he heard back, and with the attempted investigation into the attack thwarted by Wanton and Sessions and their maneuvering, we can only imagine his frustration. But when a sloop of war arrived in Newport with a package for him, it must have felt like Christmas.

King George and his advisors didn't trust the Rhode Island judiciary to handle the inquiry, and with good reason. Even an ocean away, the whole thing smelled fishy. British officials decided to sidestep the untrustworthy colonists and open their own investigation.

To that end, the Crown issued a royal proclamation

> *for the discovering and apprehending the persons who plundered and burnt the* Gaspee *schooner, and barbarously wounded and ill-treated Lieutenant William Dudingston, commander of the said schooner.*
>
> *…We are hereby graciously pleased to promise, that if any person or persons shall discover any person, or persons, concerned in the said daring and heinous offences above mentioned, so that he or they may be apprehended and brought to justice, such discoverer shall have and receive, as a reward for such discovery, upon conviction of each of the said offenders, the sum of five hundred pounds.*
>
> *And if any person or persons shall discover either of the said persons who acted as, or called themselves, or were called by their said accomplices, the head sheriff, or the captain, so that they, or either of them, may be apprehended and brought to punishment, such discoverer shall have and receive as a reward for such discovery, upon conviction of either of the said persons, the further sum five hundred pounds, over and above the sum five hundred pounds herein before promised.*

The price on John Brown's and Abraham Whipple's heads—£1,000 each—was double the *Gaspee*'s original purchase price.

The proclamation went on to say that any of the raiders who turned informant and gave up any of his fellow raiders would not only receive £500 (plus another £500 for John Brown or Abe Whipple) but "also our gracious pardon for his said offence."

Included with the royal proclamation were documents ordering the formation of a commission appointed by the Crown to investigate the attack on the *Gaspee*. Chillingly, the instruction for setting up the commission stated that its members were "entrusted with the power and authority to arrest and commit to custody such of the persons concerned…in order to the said offenders being sent to England to be tried for that offense."

If Dudingston was overstepping his authority in sending the *Fortune* to Boston for trial, transporting those accused of attacking the *Gaspee* across the ocean to England was far worse, blatantly ignoring the colony's judicial rights laid down in the royal charter over a century before. This was more than some slight offered by the obnoxious Admiral Montagu; this was an insult from King George III himself.

Montagu sent the proclamation and accompanying documents to Governor Wanton. Wanton must have been alarmed as he read them over. The only bright spot, from his point of view, was that he himself had been appointed to serve on the commission; at least he would know what the commission was up to and could throw the occasional monkey wrench into the proceedings, if needed. And it no doubt would be, as the other five men appointed to the commission were solid Tories from the surrounding colonies.

The proclamation, according to its own wording, was "printed and published, in the usual form, and affixed in the principal places of our town of Newport, and other towns in our said colony, that none may pretend ignorance."

Ignorance wasn't the problem—outrage was. According to one account, when the proclamation was hung in Newport's Market Square:

> *It had not been there more than fifteen or twenty minutes when Mr. Joseph Alpin, a distinguished lawyer, came up to see what had collected*

the crowd. Lifting his cane he struck it down and it soon mingled with the filth of the street. This patriotic act, though he gave no reason for it at the time, was prompted by his regard for the safety of his fellow citizens. It was an honorable testimony to the character of the people of this town and state that the court with its bounteous reward could get no person to inform, though all engaged were well known.

In the pages of the *Providence Gazette*, an anonymous author signing himself "Americanus" wrote a lengthy and fiery editorial:

To be, or not to be, that's the question; whether our unalienable rights and privileges are any longer worth contending for, is now to be determined. Permit me, my countrymen, to beseech you to attend to your alarming situation.

A court of inquisition, more horrid than that of Spain or Portugal, in established within this colony, to inquire into the circumstances of destroying the Gaspee schooner; and the persons who are the commissioners of this new-fangled court, are vested with most exorbitant and unconstitutional power. They are directed to summon witnesses, apprehend persons not only impeached, but even suspected! and them, and every of them, to deliver them to Admiral Montagu, who is ordered to have a ship in readiness to carry them to England, where they are to be tried.

…Is there an American, in whose breast there glows the smallest spark of public virtue, but who must be fired with indignation and resentment, against a measure so replete with the ruin of our free constitution? To be tried by one's peers, is the greatest privilege a subject can wish for; and so excellent is our constitution, that no subject shall be tried, but by his peers.

Thus are we robbed of our birth-rights, and treated with every mark of indignity, insult and contempt; and can we possibly be so supine, as not to feel ourselves firmly disposed to treat, the advocates for such horrid measures with a detestation and scorn, proportionate to their perfidy and baseness?

Upon the whole, it is more than probable, it is an almost absolute certainty, that, according to the present appearances, the state of an American subject, instead of enjoying the privileges of an Englishman, will soon be infinitely worse than that of a subject of France, Spain, Portugal, or any other the most despotic power on earth; so that, my countrymen, it behooves you, it is your indispensable duty to stand forth in the glorious cause of freedom, the dearest of all your earthly enjoyments; and, with a truly Roman spirit of liberty, either prevent the fastening of the infernal chains now forging for you, and your posterity, or nobly perish in the attempt.

Deputy Governor Sessions, along with some others, reached out to Samuel Adams for advice. Adams, though more closely associated with the Boston Tea Party, was a philosophical firebrand "whom we consider as a principal in the assertion and defense of those rightful and natural blessings," according to Sessions.

We therefore ask that you would seriously consider of this whole matter, and consult such of your friends and acquaintances as you may think fit upon it, and give us your opinion in what manner this colony had best behave in this critical situation, and how the shock that is coming upon us may by best evaded or sustained. We beg you, answer as soon as may be.

An outspoken critic of British colonial policy, the Harvard-educated Adams was then serving in the Massachusetts House of Representatives. He also worked in the family brewing business. In his younger days, he had been a tax collector but eventually lost the job, as he rarely bothered to collect any taxes. He remains a controversial figure today, seen as one of the philosopher-saints of the Revolution by some and as a master of propaganda and spin by others.

It should be noted that some historians suspect Sam Adams was Americanus, while others think it was Stephen Hopkins, himself a sharp critic of the British authorities and one of the men who joined Sessions in seeking Adams's advice.

Rhode Island had done little to earn Adams's admiration. Several years before, Sam Adams had spearheaded a nonimportation agreement, refusing to allow the import of a number of heavily taxed items ("any tea, glass, paper, or other goods commonly imported from Great Britain") until the tax on them was repealed. While some other colonies joined in the boycott, Rhode Island refused. A Boston paper of the time fumed against "the little, filthy, nasty, dirty colony of Rhode Island." But evidently Adams was willing to let bygones be bygones when Sessions and the others sought his advice. They were, after all, united in their struggle.

In his hasty response, Adams condemned the commission as "against the first principles of government and the English constitution." The commission's intention to send the accused to England "appears to me to be repugnant to the first principles of natural justice." He went on to declare, "It has ever been my opinion, that an attack upon the liberties of one colony is an attack upon the liberties of all."

In a follow-up letter a few days later, Adams warned:

> *It appears to me probable that the administration has a design to get your charter vacated. The Execution of so extraordinary a commission, unknown in your charter and abhorrent to the principles of every free government, wherein persons are appointed to enquire into offences committed against a law of another legislature, with the power of transporting the persons they shall suspect beyond the seas to be tried, would essentially change your constitution; and a silence under such a change would be construed a submission to it.*

He added:

> *I have long feared that this unhappy contest between Britain and America will end in rivers of blood; should that be the case, America I think may wash her hands in Innocence; yet it is the highest prudence to prevent if possible so dreadful a calamity…*
>
> *PS—I beg just to propose for consideration whether a circular letter from your assembly on this occasion, to those of the other colonies might*

not tend to the advantage of the general cause and of R. Island in particular; I should think it would induce each of them, at least to injoin their agents in Great Britain to represent the severity of your case in the strongest terms.

Adams's passionate and eloquent letters may not have contained as much practical advice as Sessions had hoped and, indeed, said very little the deputy governor didn't already know, but they do give voice to a vision of the colonies being united. An attack on the liberties of one was an attack on the liberties of all. That was a bold vision in the cold winter of 1772, and the flame of discontent that burned the *Gaspee* would only grow brighter and hotter in the coming months.

Chapter 10

SPIRITED OPPOSITION

After sorting out the logistics, the Royal Commission was finally called to order on January 5, 1773. The commissioners were Governor Joseph Wanton, chairman; eighty-one-year-old New York chief justice Daniel Horsmanden; New Jersey chief justice Frederick Smythe, described by a contemporary as "Loyalist by birth, education, and instinct"; Massachusetts chief justice Peter Oliver; and Judge Robert Auchmuty, who sat on the vice-admiralty court headquartered in Boston and had previously served as attorney for the defense during the Boston Massacre trials. They convened in Newport's grand Colony House, in front of which the longboats from the *St. John* and the *Liberty* had been torched not long before.

Horsmanden was not impressed. He grumbled to the Earl of Dartmouth, Hillsborough's replacement as secretary of state for the colonies, that "on my arrival…I was surprised to find that the main object of our errand was become public, which, in prudence, was to be kept secret; nevertheless, Your Lordship's letter to Governor Wanton, was published in the Boston weekly paper, and spread industriously all over New England." He was further angered when he found out that Wanton himself was responsible, but the governor countered that "he by law was obliged to communicate all dispatches from the Ministry…

The Newport Colony House still stands at the head of Washington Square today. *Author's collection.*

and sworn to do so." Horsmanden rolled his eyes. "My Lord, as to the Government (if it deserves that name), it is a downright democracy; the Governor is a mere nominal one, and therefore is a cipher, without power or authority; entirely controlled by the populace." (He actually had a point. While the royal charter of 1663 did create the office of governor, it nowhere described the governor's powers or responsibilities. Real legislative power rested with the General Assembly, with the governor being very much a figurehead.)

John Brown may have breathed a sigh of relief when he heard who was on the commission. As chairman, Wanton was in a position to minimize the damage the commission could do, and John had previously done business with Peter Oliver. Having two friendly faces on the commission could go a long way toward helping him avoid being extradited to England for trial.

The commissioners took "the usual state oaths" to discharge their duty, including pledging their loyalty to King George III. Bizarrely, among the oaths was one stating:

We do solemnly and sincerely in the presence of God profess, testify, and declare, that we do believe that, in the sacrament of the Lord's supper, there is not any transubstantiation of the elements of bread and wine into the body and blood of Christ at, or after, the consecration thereof, by any person whatsoever, and that the invocation, or adoration, of the Virgin Mary, or any other saint, and the sacrifice of the mass, as they are now used in the Church of Rome, are superstitious and idolatrous. And we do solemnly, in the presence of God, profess, testify, and declare, that we do make this declaration, and every part thereof, in the plain and ordinary sense of the words read unto us, as they are commonly understood by English Protestants, without any evasion, equivocation, or mental reservation whatsoever.

The commission advertised in the *Newport Mercury* that it had convened and "all persons who can give any information to the said commissioners, relative to the assembling, arming, and leading on of the persons who made the said attack, and the directing and preparing the same, are requested forthwith to give information thereof, to the said commissioners at the above mentioned place."

The rest of Rhode Island was watching. According to Ezra Stiles:

The commissioners sat daily, Sundays excepted, appointed two clerks, but no other officers, and committed all occurrences, letters &c to writing but all secret. The week before the commissioner's arrival, the general assembly sat at Providence, when it was deliberated what methods should be taken. A motion was made for spirited opposition, declaration of rights, denial of jurisdiction of the commissioners &c. On the whole, it was judged best to sit still for the present, till it should appear with what degree of earnestness the commissioners should proceed, and adjourned to about a fortnight, when they again assembled at E. Greenwich, by which time it began to appear that nothing very sanguinary would be attempted. And though there was some spirited talk in the assembly, yet, on the whole, it was determined to let things rest. Chief Justice Hopkins motioned for direction from the Assembly how to act in case he was applied to for apprehending persons for delivery &c, the assembly left it to his discretion. It is said, he then declared, before the assembly, both houses, that, for the purpose of transportation for trial, he would neither apprehend by his own order, nor suffer any executive officers in the colony to do it. Our Superior Court are ready to try criminals before themselves, not to send any out of the colony for trial, and in this light, must be understood, the judges offering their assistance.

Perhaps in a punctilious attempt to cross every *t* and dot every *i*, or perhaps simply to inconvenience and annoy him, Governor Wanton decided that Admiral Montagu's presence was absolutely necessary. The admiral protested that

the season of the year does not admit of my coming to Rhode Island, with my flag, and such ships as shall be necessary to assist the commissioners to my instructions, yet, if the commissioners shall think it right, and for the good of the service they are upon, that my presence is necessary, I shall be ready to set out the moment I receive such notice from them. But I flatter myself they will be able to do so, without me.

Wanton insisted, and two weeks later, Montagu made the overland journey down icy New England roads to hoist his flag aboard the *Lizard*, a twenty-eight-gun frigate anchored in Newport Harbor. He complained that the cannon of Fort George on Goat Island did not fire a salute as he made his arrival.

And the Royal Commission settled down to business.

Among the first to appear was one Stephen Gulley, a "husbandman" from Smithfield. He knew of the proclamation and of the hefty reward being offered for information. Though not involved himself, he did recall some loose talk from over the summer. Saul Ramsdale, a Providence shoemaker, had seemed to know something. Lured by the reward being dangled in front of him, Gulley sought out the shoemaker, finding him at home, just over the Massachusetts border. Taking him aside, Gulley asked him what he knew of the attack on the *Gaspee*.

Who said he knew anything? Ramsdale asked cautiously.

Gulley wouldn't say but promised to "be a good friend to him" if he told what he knew.

Ramsdale confessed that he "did know something about the thing. That he knew the heads of the gang that went down the river with that intention; that he saw two men with guns under their arms; and one of them swore a very high oath that he would be revenged upon the affair he was going upon, before he returned."

According to Gulley, Ramsdale said he was invited to join the attack but refused, "being faint-hearted and discouraged."

Gulley pressed the hapless shoemaker—did he know any names? Weren't some of the Brown brothers involved?

Yes, Ramsdale agreed. But he didn't know which; he could "not remember that he mentioned his Christian name."

Ramsdale went on to estimate the size of the raiding party as "something upwards" of three hundred men. He begged Gulley not to reveal him to the authorities.

Gulley set off to Newport to offer what he now knew to the commission and hopefully collect his reward. He stopped at a tavern in Portsmouth for some supper. Thomas Aylesbury, another patron, took a seat next to him in the taproom and whispered, "My friend, I believe you are upon some bad design, as I understood by your talk you are going to Newport to give information about the burning of the *Gaspee*."

Gulley replied that it was nobody's business but his own.

Aylesbury said, "There were about twenty armed men in the road, one of them with two brass pistols who…were come to take him alive or dead and carry him back to Providence."

The landlord, Joseph Borden, then spoke up, saying that the mob outside would probably tear the house down to get to Gulley. He offered to sneak Gulley past the mob of wild "Indians, with brass pistols," and together they stole carefully through the night until coming to another road, where Borden left him. Gulley was evidently shaken enough by the whole episode that he sought shelter aboard the *Lizard* when he finally arrived in Newport and waited there to testify before the commission.

When summoned to testify before the commission, Joseph Borden shrugged the whole thing off, stating that Gulley "appeared to be in liquor" and "that he did not know, neither has any reason to believe, that there were any Indians in the road leading to Newport; and…supposed that Aylesbury told his story to Gulley, with no other design but to frighten him." But he did admit to sneaking Gulley out of the house, perhaps just to get rid of him.

What are we to make of this story? There certainly could have been a gang looking to prevent Gulley from reaching Newport, seeking to intimidate the would-be informant into silence or worse. Gangs had searched for Dudingston when he was still ashore in Pawtuxet, so obviously Rhode Islanders didn't hesitate to resort to such extreme measures. If it happened once, it must have happened more than once. We are left to wonder how many more similar stories there may be that we don't know about.

Joseph Borden, of course, in dismissing the talk of "Indians" waiting in the road with brass pistols, observed the code of silence, like so many others throughout the colony.

Aaron Briggs came ashore for the first time in six months and was brought before the commission. He repeated his story of the nighttime raid he had been dragged into. Patrick Earle, the *Gaspee* sailor who sat in the longboat with Aaron and Dudingston as they rowed away from the grounded schooner, identified him as one of the raiders before the commission. Earle further stated "that one of the people said, 'Potter, it is the best way to set the men on shore, for that it was not their fault, but the officers.'"

A man named Daniel Vaughan appeared before the commissioners next. Over the summer, he had been part of a salvage operation "taking out some old iron from the wreck of the *Gaspee*, and afterwards going down to Newport" to report his progress to Captain Linzee. According to his testimony, when he came aboard the *Beaver*:

> *I saw a mulatto fellow under the forecastle, in irons.*
>
> *I said unto him, "So you are one of the rogues that have been burning the* Gaspee.*"*
>
> *He replied, "He never saw her, nor knew any thing about her."*
>
> *Then I asked him what he came here for.*
>
> *He answered, "His master had used him badly, and he was determined to leave him."*

Vaughan related that it was only after Linzee ordered Aaron to be whipped that "he began to declare he knew some of the people that burnt the *Gaspee*, and that Simeon Potter, John Brown and others (whose names I have forgot) were concerned therein."

His testimony that Aaron had at first denied all knowledge of the *Gaspee*, and only began naming names under the threat of flogging, cast further doubt on the veracity of Aaron's original statement.

But who was Daniel Vaughan? Daniel Vaughan was listed as a lieutenant serving aboard Simeon Potter's privateer, *Prince Charles of Lorraine*, on the South American voyage—the infamous voyage on which Potter had looted the local church. More recently, he had been the commander of the cannon crew at Fort George that, at Stephen Hopkins's order, had fired over a dozen shots at the *St. John* in 1764.

Vaughan's history pretty clearly shows where his loyalties were, both political and personal. He might have been recruited by Governor Wanton, Darius Sessions or perhaps even his old captain, Simeon Potter himself, but he was a man on a mission—to further discredit Aaron Briggs. We can almost imagine him winking to Wanton on his way out of the courtroom.

June 9, the night the *Gaspee* was attacked, also marked the end of a court term. It was common custom for the gentlemen of the law to spend the evening unwinding together while talking shop, and Sabin's Tavern was evidently a popular spot for doing do. The commission obtained the names of a handful of the lawyers who were there that night and summoned them all. Surely they would recognize how serious the matter was. Surely one of them would talk.

But every one of the men refused to appear. Each said he knew nothing of the affair and nothing unusual had happened at Sabin's Tavern that night. Some of them did hear a drum being beaten out in the street but dismissed it as "a number of boys met together…to divert themselves." One of them added that he "hoped they were not designed for any mischief."

One of the lawyers, John Andrews, was especially unable to attend. Not only did he have nothing material to tell the commissioners, but he went on to explain, "I have been confined for a week past, with a swelling in my hand, which hath rendered me unable to stir out of doors."

Clearly, these men were joining in the conspiracy of silence. No one at Sabin's that night could have failed to know what was going on—with John Brown laying out plans and barking orders and men casting bullets in the kitchen, as more and more men arrived by the minute. They knew what was going on that night, but they kept their mouths shut and, in doing so, perjured themselves before the Royal Commission.

The whole investigation was grinding to a halt. They had uncovered no solid evidence allowing them to arrest the rumored ringleaders. In three weeks, they had encountered evasion, obfuscation, excuses and outright falsehood. Montagu was anxious to return to Boston, and the other commissioners had business to attend to back home in their respective colonies. It was decided to adjourn until May. Perhaps the spring thaw would bring something forth.

Samuel Adams had been an early advocate of the establishment of Committees of Correspondence in the colonies. These committees would keep one another informed of recent developments, create a sense of unity among the colonists and help present a united front against what was seen as growing British tyranny. Such committees had been formed in response to specific problems before—one had been formed in resistance to the Stamp Act back in 1764—but Adams and others saw a need for permanent, better-organized committees with broader reach. One was established in Boston, and other colonies slowly began to follow suit.

In March 1773, while the Royal Commission was still adjourned, the Virginia House of Burgesses—the colony's General Assembly—formed "a Committee of Correspondence and Inquiry," with Thomas Jefferson and Patrick Henry among its members.

The committee stated that "His Majesty's faithful subjects have been much disturbed by various rumors and reports of proceedings tending to deprive them of their ancient, legal, and constitutional rights," rights that stretched back to the Magna Carta. As a committee of correspondence, they were "to obtain the most early and authentic intelligence of all such acts, and resolutions of the British Parliament, or proceedings of the administration as may relate to, or affect the British colonies in America, and do keep and maintain a correspondence with our sister colonies, respecting these important considerations; and the result of such proceedings, from time to time, to lay before the House."

The House of Burgesses commented specifically on recent events in Rhode Island, casting a harsh eye on the doings of the Royal Commission. The new Committee of Correspondence was "to inform themselves particularly of the principles and authority on which was constituted a court of inquiry said to have been lately held in Rhode Island, with power to transport persons accused of offenses committed in America, to places beyond the sea, to be tried."

Thomas Jefferson himself later recalled:

> *Nothing of particular excitement occurring for a considerable time; our countrymen seemed to fall into a state of insensibility to our situation. The duty on tea had not yet been repealed, and the Declaratory Act of a right in the British parliament to bind us by their laws in all cases whatsoever, still suspended over us. But a court of inquiry held in Rhode Island in 1772, with a power to send persons to England to be tried for offences committed here was considered at our session of the spring*

> *of 1773 as demanding attention…We were all sensible that the most urgent of all measures was that of coming to an understanding with all the other colonies to consider the British claims as a common cause to all, and to produce a unity of action, and for this purpose that a committee of correspondence in each colony would be the best instrument for intercommunication, and that their first measure would probably be to propose a meeting of deputies from every colony at some central place, who should be charged with the direction of the measures which should be taken by all. We therefore drew up the resolutions.*

Rhode Island formed its own committee two months later, in May. Stephen Hopkins and Moses Brown served, along with others. The committeemen were to open communications with the other colonial legislatures "relating to the preservation of the rights of the colonies."

The Committees of Correspondence were a major factor, and arguably *the* factor, in forging a united colonial identity, as they moved away from seeing themselves as British colonists and thinking of themselves as something different—as Americans. The Committees of Correspondence would soon lead to the formation of the Constitutional Convention in Philadelphia, where the thirteen colonies would declare their independence from Great Britain on July 4, 1776.

And the burning of the *Gaspee* was a big step on that road.

When the Royal Commission finally did reconvene in June 1773, it was more of the same. *Gaspee* sailors described the attack, men came forward to cast further aspersions on Aaron Briggs's story and others brought before the commissioners denied all knowledge. Chief Justice Smythe wanted to broaden the scope of the inquiry to include the 1764 attack on the *St. John*, but Wanton, as chairman, wouldn't allow it. Wanton also engaged in some creative stage management designed to protect those involved. For instance, he agreed to allow Rufus Greene to send in a written statement detailing the seizure of the *Fortune*, rather than testify in person before the commission. Rufus had been aboard the *Gaspee* that night, and Wanton could not run the risk that he might be recognized by any of the *Gaspee* crewmen who happened to be at the Colony House if Rufus appeared before the commission.

After another few weeks of getting nowhere, the commissioners threw in the towel. They issued a lengthy final report to the king, reeking of failure. Clearly, there had been a very real attack carried out on the king's schooner, but that was about as much as they had been able to discover with any certainty.

There had long been a question of whether Newport had actually been the base of operations for the attackers. But Newport's distance from the scene and the relatively short amount of time between the *Gaspee* running aground and the actual attack "take away all possibility of the inhabitants of the town being instrumental in or privy to the destruction of her; nor have we any evidence, even of the slightest kind, to induce suspicion to the contrary."

The search for the men behind the attack had come to nothing: "In the part of our duty contained under the inquiry into the assembling, arming, and leading on the people to attack the *Gaspee*, also the concerting and preparing the same, we have been particularly attentive. But after our utmost efforts, we are not able to discover any evidence of either."

"After exerting ourselves to the utmost of our abilities to collect evidence against the persons concerned in burning the *Gaspee* and wounding the lieutenant, and judging that we had got all there was any probability of obtaining," they turned to a lengthy discussion of Aaron Briggs and his testimony. "Touching the depositions of Aaron, the negro, we humbly conceive it our duty to declare to Your Majesty, that the conduct of Captain Linzee tended too strongly to exert from a weak or wicked mind declarations not strictly true…and therefore we are most humbly of the opinion, no credit is due to said Aaron's testimony."

In conclusion, the final report solemnly declared: "May it please Your Majesty, the civil magistrates being entrusted with the power of apprehending and committing, and having determined against both, upon no evidence before them, and there being no probability of our procuring any more further light on the subject determines our inquiry."

With the filing of their final report, the Royal Commission disbanded; the commissioners went home and tried to put the whole sorry business behind them.

John Brown, Abe Whipple and Simeon Potter must have been the happiest men in the colony.

They had gotten away with it.

Chapter 11

AFTERMATH

The men who burned the *Gaspee* were local heroes and could once again safely walk the streets with heads held high. Broadsides celebrating the attack began to circulate. One such song is attributed to a Captain Swan of Bristol, said to have been among the raiders. The top of the sheet shows the British arms, supported by the lion and unicorn, upside down, with the motto "King George's Crown—Turn'd Upside Down!"

'Twas in the reign of George the Third,
Our public peace was much disturbed
By ships of war that came and laid
Within our ports, to stop our trade.

Seventeen hundred and seventy-two,
In Newport Harbor lay a crew
That played the parts of pirates there,
The sons of freedom could not bear.

Sometimes they weighed and gave them chase,
Such actions, sure, were very base.

'TWAS in the reign of George the Third
Our public peace was much disturb'd,
By Ships of War that come and laid
Within our ports to stop our trade.

In Seventeen Hundred Seventy Two,
In Newport harbour lay a crew,
That play'd the parts of Pirates there,
The Sons of Freedom could not bare.

Sometimes they'd weigh and give them chace,
Such actions sure were very base ;
No honest Coasters could pass by,
But what they would let some shot fly.

And did provoke to high degree
Those true born Sons of Liberty,
So that they could no longer bare
Those Sons of Belial staying there.

But 'twas not long 'fore it fell out,
That William Dodd'ngton so stout,
Commander of the GASPEE Tender,
Which he has reason to remember.

Because as people do insert,
He almost had his just desert ;
Here on the tenth day of last June,
Between the hours of twelve and one—

Did chace the Sloop call'd the Hannah,
Of whom one Linsey was commander ;
They dog'd her up to Providence sound
And there the rascal got a ground.

The news of it flew that very day,
That they on Nanquit Point did lay,
That night about half after ten
Some Narraganset Indianmen—

Being Sixty-Four, if I remember,
Which made this stout Coxcomb surrender :
And what was best of all their tricks,
They in his britch a ball did fix !

They set the men upon the land,
And burnt her up we understand :
Which thing provok'd the King so high
He said those men should surely die.

So if he could find them out,
The hangman he'll employ no doubt,
For he has declared in his passion
He'll have them tried a new fashion.

Now for to find those people out,
King George has offered very stout,
One Thousand Pounds to find out one
That wounded William Doddingston !

One Thousand more he says he'll spare,
For those who say they sheriffs were :
One Thousand more there doth remain
For to find out the Leader's name.

Likewise Five Hundred Pounds per man,
Of any one of all the clan,
But let him try his utmost skill
I am apt to think he never will
Find out any of those hearts of gold,
Though he should offer fifty fold.

Printed No. 25, High Street, Providence, with 200 other kinds of Songs

"King George's Crown—Turn'd Upside Down!" One of several ballads written shortly after the attack. *Courtesy Brown University.*

> *No honest coaster could pass by*
> *But what they would let some shot fly;*

> *And did provoke, to high degree,*
> *Those true born sons of liberty;*

So that they could no longer bear
Those sons of Belial staying there.

But 'twas not long 'fore it fell out,
That William Dudingston, so stout,
Commander of the "Gaspee" tender,
Which he has reason to remember,

Because, as people do assert,
He almost had his just desert;
Here, on the tenth day of last June,
Betwixt the hours of twelve and one,

Did chase the sloop, called the "Hannah,"
Of whom one Lindsay was commander.
They dogged her up Providence Sound,
And there the rascal got aground.

The news of it flew that very day
That they on Namquit Point did lay.
That night after half past ten
Some Narragansett Indian men,

Being sixty-four, if I remember,
Which made the stout coxcomb surrender;
And what was best of all their tricks,
They in his breech a ball did fix;

Then set the men upon the land,
And burnt her up, we understand;
Which thing provoked the King so high
He said those men shall surely die;

So if he could but find them out,
The hangman he'll employ, no doubt;
For he's declared, in his passion,
He'll have them tried a new fashion,

Now, for to find these people out,
King George has offered very stout,
One thousand pounds to find out one
That wounded William Dudingston.

One thousand more, he says he'll spare,
For those who say sheriffs were;
One thousand more there doth remain
For to find out the leader's name;

Likewise, five hundred pounds per man
For any one of all the clan.
But let him try his utmost skill,
I'm apt to think he never will
Find out any of those hearts of gold,
Though he should offer fifty fold.

Interestingly, the song backs up the idea, popular in Bristol, that the attackers disguised themselves as Indians.

On April 19, 1775, lobsterbacks marched on the town of Concord, Massachusetts, with orders "to seize and destroy…all military stores" that had been stockpiled by the Minutemen and to round up and arrest all Patriot leaders, including Samuel Adams and John Hancock. The Minutemen, having received advanced warning, had moved their supplies and were ready when the lobsterbacks reached Lexington at sunrise. While debate still continues over which side fired it, "the shot heard 'round the world" echoed across Lexington Common, and the Revolution began.

Rhode Island moved to join the fight a few days later when the General Assembly called up fifteen hundred troops, some to defend the colony and others to reinforce the rebels in Boston. Governor Wanton, a man who had confounded the Royal Commission and done his best to preserve the Rhode Island charter, regretted the descent into open hostilities. He, along with Darius Sessions, formally objected to the raising of troops. "Such a measure will be attended with the most fatal consequences to our charter privileges" and will "involve the country in all the horrors of civil war."

When Wanton refused to sign off on the General Assembly's call to arms, he was branded a Loyalist and removed from office.

John Brown had always been a businessman first and a Patriot second, and war is always good for business. John immediately struck a deal to supply the new Rhode Island army with flour, knowing, years before Napoleon, that an army travels on its stomach. Putting his career as a smuggler to good use, John set sail for Newport in two sloops, the *Diana* and the *Abigail*, planning to pick up the flour he needed and sneak it past British authorities.

But Newport was in chaos. Since November of the previous year, a Royal Navy squadron under the command of Captain Sir James Wallace had been anchored in Newport Harbor. When it came to harassing colonists, Wallace made Dudingston look like a rank amateur, and his flagship, the twenty-gun frigate *Rose*, was bigger and more powerful than the little *Gaspee* had ever been. Indeed, Wallace had the frigate's cannon aimed at Newport and let it be known that he might, at any moment, choose to pound the city to rubble.

This was the beginning of the British occupation of Newport. Over the course of a frigid winter, the British would tear down half the city's houses for firewood, chop down most of the trees and steal every book in the Redwood Library and Athenaeum. Its citizens, including Ezra Stiles, evacuated in droves. Newport would never fully recover from the occupation, never regain its position as the colony's leading city, and would soon be eclipsed by Providence.

When John Brown arrived, the situation was not as bad as it would later become. But for John personally, it was far worse than he knew. Metcalfe Bowler, speaker of the General Assembly and the man who had signed Aaron Briggs's arrest warrant, was a political operator (some called him a spy) playing both sides. He had tipped the British off about John's mission. When John arrived in Newport that day, planning to be gone before anyone even noticed him, Wallace was waiting. John was arrested, and the *Diana* was taken as a tender for the *Rose*. John was sent to Boston as a prisoner aboard his own ship, the *Abigail*.

The *Newport Mercury* protested, "Mr. Brown was sent off…to be carried to Admiral Graves in Boston, without having a single reason given for his being thus seized and carried out of this colony, contrary to all law, equity, and justice."

But of course everyone knew why John was under arrest. Smuggling flour to supply the new rebel army was just an excuse. Everyone from Wallace on down knew that John had been the leader of the raid on the *Gaspee*, and Wallace intended to succeed where the Royal Commission had failed. Under the Intolerable Acts, another round of punitive legislation passed by Parliament, John could and probably would be sent to England for trial and, if found guilty, executed.

His brother Moses traveled to Boston and, amazingly, managed to talk his way into a meeting with General Thomas Gage, commander of the British forces in North America. As a plain-spoken, pacifist Quaker, Moses looked like anything but a fiery Patriot, and that may have helped put Gage somewhat at ease.

Moses spent a few long days being shuttled back and forth between generals, admirals and judges, seeking to negotiate his brother's freedom. When he finally did get to see John aboard the ship where he was being held captive, "He was as glad to see me as he ever was."

Gage had known from the start that he had nothing to hold John on, and after what must have been the longest week of John's life, Gage released him on one condition—that the brothers would lobby the Rhode Island General Assembly to plead with the Massachusetts Patriots for peace with Great Britain. Gage had them sign a pledge to that effect and, upon obtaining their signatures, released John, ordered the return of the *Diana* and the *Abigail*, issued Wallace a formal reprimand for his conduct and even slipped John some cash.

Upon returning to Providence, John kept his word and spoke eloquently before the General Assembly. "Although the sword has been drawn and the scabbard as yet seems to be lost, I am not out of hopes that the latter may be found and the former returned to its usual rest and quiet," he said.

The scabbard, of course, was long lost, and nothing could be done to stop the inevitable slide toward Revolution.

Many years later, on that one occasion when he spoke to his grandson about his involvement in the attack, John Brown confided that he "afterwards deeply regretted this affair, as foolhardy in itself, and resulting in so much needless apprehension to himself and family. For a long time he was accustomed to sleep away from home, lest he should be arrested in the night." The grandson, John Brown Francis, added, "The first booming of the guns at Lexington and Concord filled his mind with gladness. He was a stranger himself to fear, but he rejoiced when the fears and anxieties of others were merged in the open contest now commenced. History has given to the leader in this Rhode Island enterprise the fame which he so richly deserves."

Abraham Whipple went on to serve as commodore of the Rhode Island navy (both ships!). He was later commissioned as a captain in the Continental navy and placed in command of a twenty-four-gun frigate, the *Columbus*. On a mission to steal a number of cannon from Fort George on Goat Island, he fell afoul of Captain Sir James Wallace, who wanted Whipple, the "captain" of the *Gaspee* expedition, at least as badly as he wanted John Brown, the "sheriff."

Once again, as so often happens in the story of the *Gaspee* and its aftermath, the two rivals squared off in letters, airing their grievances in writing. Wallace threatened, "You, Abraham Whipple, on the 10th of June, 1772, burned His Majesty's vessel, the *Gaspee*, and I will hang you at the yard arm."

To which Whipple replied with a chortle, "Sir: Always catch a man before you hang him."

Whipple had a successful career as a naval officer during the Revolution. Placed in command of three ships, he attacked a British convoy off the Newfoundland coast. Quickly running up a British flag, Whipple easily sidled up to the convoy before attacking and taking eleven ships as prizes.

He was eventually captured and only released upon giving his word that he would take no further part in the Revolution against Great Britain. He kept his oath and took up farming.

He is remembered today as a Patriot. A number of U.S. Navy ships have been named in his honor, and it seems that nearly every city and town in the state has a Whipple Street, Avenue, Lane or similar roadway named after him.

He is buried in Ohio, far from home.

We lose track of Aaron Briggs after the final adjournment of the Royal Commission. Like so many others, he vanishes back into the mists of history. Presumably, he went back to work on the Thurston family farm for the remainder of his indenture, finally leaving upon reaching age twenty-four. What he did with the rest of his life is anybody's guess.

There is, however, one tantalizing possibility. In 1832, a seventy-six-year-old man named Aaron Briggs applied for a pension for his service as a private in the Revolution. There is no record of his race, and his memory of his service was hazy, but he remembered fighting in the Battle of Rhode Island, the state's lone and not very impressive military action during the fight for independence.

He could not remember the regiment in which he served, but one of the units that fought in that battle was the First Rhode Island Regiment, widely acknowledged as the first-ever black regiment. While not everyone serving in the unit was African-American, the majority certainly were. A seventy-six-year-old man in 1832 would have been sixteen in 1772, which is the age most people estimated for Aaron at the time.

Is this pensioner the same Aaron Briggs who was dragged along on the nighttime raid on the *Gaspee*? We can't say for certain, but it seems pretty likely. It is interesting and perhaps even heartening to note that the pensioner signed his name to his paperwork, whereas the teenaged Aaron Briggs signed his statements with an X.

Somewhere along the line, he had learned to write.

Dr. John Mawney and Ephraim Bowen both went on to serve as colonels in the Revolution.

Mawney inherited some wealth and further prospered by investing in various financial and mercantile ventures; it was said that he never practiced medicine to a great extent, apparently preferring to spend his time reading Greek and Roman poets instead. He married twice and was evidently something of a rake, as it was noted, "He suffered greatly in the public esteem, on account of his bold unblushing irreverence and infidelity."

Bowen made considerable money distilling rum, and one of his still houses yet stands, though it was moved from its original location and is now a private residence. He likewise married twice and bought a home in Warwick, chosen because, from one window, it overlooked Namquit Point, since renamed Gaspee Point.

Both men were honored in a parade on July 4, 1826, celebrating the fiftieth anniversary of American independence. Alongside over one hundred veterans, Mawney and Bowen rode in a carriage, waving to the crowds, along with Benjamin Page and Turpin Smith, the only other raiders still living. They sat under a hand-painted silk banner bearing their names and an image of the burning *Gaspee*. According to the *Providence Journal*:

> *It was a matter of most interesting association and recollection, to witness these four surviving "lads," who burnt the* Gaspee *(as the orator so happily termed them), at the end of fifty-four years, riding in a splendid equipage, and receiving the award of a republican triumph, for a deed, the commission of which, at that time, had well nigh caused them to ride in a cart to Execution Dock, or to be drawn on a hurdle to Tyburn, for high treason; an event they anticipated as vastly more likely*

A sketch of the elderly Ephraim Bowen. Nel Slocum, a Pawtuxet resident who remembered Bowen, wrote, "He was about five feet-nine and he wore small clothes, in the old fashion. His pants came down to his knees and he wore stockings and shoes with big silver buckles in the tops…But he always walked mighty stiff and erect and he was 'Col. Bowen' all right. We boys were always afraid of him." *Courtesy Henry A.L. Brown.*

than that in 1826, the jubilee of American freedom, they should become the time honored objects of the greatest interest to an immense concourse of citizens, thronging the streets and crowding to the altar of freedom, to offer up the sacrifices and thanksgivings of a great, prosperous and free people. These four veterans Col. Ephraim Bowen, Capt. Benjamin Page, Col. John Mawney, and Capt. Turpin Smith, are among our most respected citizens; and on this occasion, the spirit that first animated them in 1772, seemed to kindle anew in their still vigorous frames. We believe, from the present ages of these veterans, they were all not over twenty years of age, at the time of the attack upon the Gaspee.

Stephen Hopkins remained active in Rhode Island politics for years and represented the colony at the Constitutional Convention in Philadelphia. On July 4, 1776, along with Newport's William Ellery, Hopkins signed the Declaration of Independence. Aged and probably suffering from Parkinson's, he used both hands to sign. Passing the pen to the next delegate, he said, "Though my hand does shake, my heart does not."

He probably took a quiet satisfaction in knowing that Rhode Island had renounced its allegiance to the British Empire two months before, on May 4, a day that would be celebrated as Rhode Island Independence Day for decades to come.

Sabin's Tavern no longer stands. Various alterations and renovations were made, including the addition of a third story and an ell, and it was bought and sold several times before being foreclosed upon in the 1870s. It was finally torn down in 1891, but not before the room

209 Williams Street, the Gaspee House, where the room from Sabin's Tavern was carefully attached. *Courtesy Providence Public Library.*

Photo of the Gaspee Room. The engraving on the mantel reads: "In this room June 9 1772 was formed the plan for the destruction of the British naval schooner 'Gaspee.'" *Courtesy Providence Public Library.*

in which John Brown had gathered his men on that fateful night was detached and moved to 209 Williams Street, where it was attached to the house. The owner of 209, Mr. Talbot, had purchased the old tavern at auction, though not the land upon which it sat, and hoped to preserve this piece of history.

The Daughters of the American Revolution placed a plaque on the outside of the home and maintained "The *Gaspee* Room" as a sort of shrine and showplace for a number of years. Plans to convert it into a museum never came together, and today 209 Williams Street is a private residence divided into rental units. One fortunate renter can now entertain guests and do the Sunday crossword in the very room where John Brown and his cohorts made history on the eve of the Revolution.

William Dudingston, later promoted to captain, returned to North America in 1776, arriving at Halifax to take command of the sloop of war *Senegal*. He would go on to command several other ships during the war and eventually retire as an admiral, though this may have been more a combination of longevity and being wounded in action; there is nothing in what we know of his seemingly unremarkable service record to suggest that he was promoted on merit alone.

He married in 1802 and retired to his native Fife, in Scotland. He fathered four children before dying in 1817, at age seventy-six.

Part of the musket ball was never removed from his body, and according to one unsourced account, it "worked its way down near the right knee, rendering him lame all his life."

The *Gaspee* herself is long gone; not even a wreck remains. Occasionally, someone will claim to have found her, but upon further inspection, the discoveries have all proven to be overenthusiastic misidentifications.

Ephraim Bowen was said to have carved four canes from wood he recovered from the *Gaspee*; perhaps he rowed out to the abandoned wreck while it was still there. Two of these canes survive today; one is in private hands, and the other is in the collection of the Rhode Island Historical Society and on display at the John Brown House Museum on Benefit Street.

The Royal Navy christened a second ship, a brig, as the *Gaspee* and even sent the new ship briefly to Newport during the Revolution. Many colonists must have contemplated lighting this new one on fire, too.

In 1770, American agitation eventually led to the repeal of the Townshend Acts, removing a number of heavy taxes that had been enforced on a variety of articles. A tax on tea, however, remained in force, much to the consternation of the American colonists. In November 1773, three cargo ships belonging to the East India Company arrived in Boston Harbor

Boston can have its tea party. In 1876, Rhode Islanders created a teacup and saucer set commemorating the destruction of the *Gaspee*, made, ironically, in England. *Courtesy Henry A.L. Brown.*

with a shipment of tea aboard. One of the ships, coincidentally, was named the *Beaver*, though she was not the same ship as the sloop of war once stationed at Newport.

Samuel Adams saw an opportunity and raised a public outcry to send the tea back to England rather than unload the cargo and pay the tax on it. On December 16, 1773, the Sons of Liberty, halfheartedly disguised as Indians, boarded the merchant ships and dumped over three hundred chests of tea into Boston Harbor.

Every schoolchild is taught that the famous Boston Tea Party was the first act of open resistance to British rule, the first pushback against taxation without representation. The men disguised as Indians, throwing chests of hated British tea overboard, is one of the most iconic images of the Revolutionary War to this very day—despite the fact that the *Gaspee* was burned eighteen months earlier.

On March 2, 1775, Providence would stage its own tea party, burning a quantity of tea outside the market house, but it must be admitted that the event doesn't have nearly the panache of torching a schooner and wounding her commander.

For many years, Rhode Islanders were inconsistent in their appreciation of the burning of the *Gaspee*. The nineteenth century saw occasional celebrations of the event, one being held in 1875, three years after the actual centennial of the event itself. There was some grumbling that in 1872 perhaps people had simply forgotten about it.

The year 1876 saw the opening of the five-story Victorian Gothic *Gaspee* Building on Westminster Street, across from the Providence Journal Building.

The twentieth century proved kinder. Back when telephone exchanges still had names instead of numerical prefixes, the GAspee exchange (421 today) covered much of downtown Providence. The Rhode Island Statehouse rises atop Smith Hill; probably the best view of the building is to be had from the Gaspee Street side.

The 1960s rode roughshod over historic preservation in Warwick, as notable buildings were demolished with a battle cry of "urban renewal." In 1965, a group of civic leaders, spearheaded by David Stackhouse, a radio broadcaster and chairman of the Warwick Heritage Committee, organized a new celebration called Gaspee Day. Stackhouse's intention was not only to remind people of the significance of the *Gaspee* episode but also to raise awareness of historic preservation generally before any more significant sites were lost. Stackhouse was a man who knew how to get things done, and in true Rhode Island fashion, he knew who to talk to and who to get involved in his plans.

The first Gaspee Day parade was held in 1966. The parade's grand marshal was ninety-two-year-old Walter Whipple, a descendent of Abraham Whipple. He sported a tricorn hat and carried a staff made up of fragments of wood said to have come from the *Gaspee*—Rhode Island's version of the True Cross. Cannon were fired off, church bells tolled and concerts and boat races were held in conjunction with the celebration.

1772   *First Annual Gaspee Day*   1966

The Burning of the Gaspee - Taylor

PICTURE COURTESY OF FIREMEN'S MUTUAL INSURANCE COMPANY

The announcement of the first annual Gaspee Day, which would soon become Gaspee Days. *Courtesy Henry A.L. Brown.*

Stackhouse's campaign for historic preservation, with the *Gaspee* as its centerpiece, accomplished more than just throwing a grand party. It is largely due to him and his allies and supporters that a sewage pumping plant proposed for Namquit Point, now renamed Gaspee Point, was never built.

It was soon clear that Gaspee Day was such a success that it would have to become Gaspee Days. Today, Gaspee Days is a major event in the Rhode Island calendar. Summer means Gaspee Days as thousands flock to events scattered over several weeks—a popular arts and crafts show, a road race, a colonial encampment peopled by costumed interpreters and, of course, the famous parade, all culminating in the ceremonial burning of a tiny replica of the British schooner.

For many years, there has been good-natured debate among historians as to how carefully orchestrated the attack on the *Gaspee* actually was. One school of thought maintains that John Brown and his cohorts took advantage of the opportunity fate placed in their way. There must have been months of loose talk about how Dudingston should be dealt with, but we don't know that plans for an attack were laid out in advance. But when the *Gaspee* ran aground, it was simply too good to miss. It wouldn't be the first time in history that circumstances lined up just right. Attacking the schooner was a crime of opportunity.

But an opposing view holds that the *Gaspee* and her crew fell victim to a carefully planned conspiracy that had been laid out long in advance. Advocates of this theory raise some interesting points. John Brown and his brother Moses had run aground on Namquit Point one June night a dozen years before and knew all about the dangerous shallows and how long it would take for the tide to come in, so he may have factored this in when scheduling the date for the attack. It is pointed out that there is no mention of Lindsay having cargo or passengers aboard the *Hannah*, suggesting that he might not have had any, making the ship lighter and faster and reducing her draft; sitting higher in the water would make her more able to navigate the hazards around Namquit Point and lure the *Gaspee* to her doom. The moon had set by 12:45 a.m., the time of the attack, so it may have been specifically scheduled to take place under cover of darkness. The speed with which the raiders organized their expedition is also cited as a factor in favor of a carefully planned conspiracy to destroy the schooner.

Some historians theorize that the attack on the *Gaspee* may have been an attempt to serve Dudingston with an arrest warrant for the *Fortune* debacle; the trick would be to get him off the ship and onto dry land, where he could be served or arrested.

While these latter two reinterpretations seem to be overly elaborate explanations of what happened, they do offer some interesting food for thought.

While long neglected and inconsistently observed, today the burning of the *Gaspee* has become a point of civic pride for many Rhode Islanders.

Right: A commemorative *Gaspee* coin. *Courtesy Henry A.L. Brown.*

Below: A one-pound package of Gaspee chocolate from a local company, circa 1930. The image is based on the McNevin painting. *Courtesy Henry A.L. Brown.*

The men involved, forced to keep their secret for much of their lives, are today celebrated as heroes, even if they were in reality more opportunistic than they were patriotic.

Regardless, the burning of the *Gaspee* serves as a bright reminder to all Rhode Islanders that history didn't just happen in Boston, Philadelphia or New York. Events of real historic import, with far-reaching consequences and connections, happened right here in our own state, in Warwick and

Pawtuxet. It also reminds us that those who make history aren't always square-jawed idealists, and they don't need to be—sometimes they're slave traders and rumrunners. But whoever they were and whatever their motives might have been, they are part of our history, and we should remember them and keep their memories green.

GLOSSARY

Eighteenth-century naval terms are arcane, byzantine and downright frustrating. This should ease the reader's confusion and also remind you of some terms you should remember from history class.

BRIG: Two-masted, square-rigged ship. Not to be confused with a brigantine.

BRIGANTINE: Two-masted ship, square-rigged on the foremast and fore-and-aft-rigged on the mainmast.

CHARTER: Document issued by the king, authorizing and creating a colony, serving as the colony's founding document. Occasionally referred to as the colony's "constitution."

FORE-AND-AFT-RIGGED: With triangular sails arranged parallel to the ship's hull, running from the fore (front) to the aft (rear).

FRIGATE: A fast, midsized warship, generally a three-masted square-rigged ship with twenty guns or more.

INTOLERABLE ACTS (also called the Coercive Acts): Legislation sharply curtailing colonial self-government.

LOBSTERBACK: Derogatory period term for a soldier in the British regular army, so called because of the bright red coat that was part of the uniform or, according to some, for the scars of being flogged in punishment; today, we call them redcoats.

PRIVATEER: A privately owned ship authorized by a government to attack the ships of rival nations. The term also applies to the captain of such a ship.

PRIZE: A captured enemy ship.

SCHOONER: A light, two-masted fore-and-aft-rigged vessel used extensively in North America.

SHIP OF THE LINE: Large, three-masted, square-rigged warship of first, second or third rate (carrying sixty-four or more guns).

SLOOP: A light, single-masted fore-and-aft-rigged vessel.

SLOOP OF WAR: A sloop carrying ten or more guns on a single deck.

SQUARE-RIGGED: With square sails running perpendicular to the ship's hull.

TORY/LOYALIST: A colonist who remained loyal to Great Britain.

TOWNSHEND ACTS: Yet another unpopular round of oppressive tax and custom legislation, passed in 1766 and sponsored by Chancellor to the exchequer Charles Townsend.

TRIANGLE TRADE: A business venture where New England rum was traded for African slaves, who were then traded or sold for West Indian molasses and sugar, which was brought back to New England to make more rum.

VICE-ADMIRALTY COURT: A juryless judicial court specifically for handling maritime matters.

SELECTED BIBLIOGRAPHY

While many sources were consulted, these proved to be the most helpful.

Bartlett, John Russell. *A History of the Destruction of His Britannic Majesty's Schooner* Gaspee *in Narragansett Bay, on 10th June, 1772*. Providence, RI: A. Crawford Greene, 1861.

Bryant, Samuel W. "HMS Gaspee—The Court Martial." *Rhode Island History* 25, no. 3 (July 1966).

———. "Rhode Island Justice—1775 Vintage." *Rhode Island History* 26, no. 3 (July 1967).

Haley, John Williams. *The Old Stone Bank History of Rhode Island*. 4 vols. Providence, RI: Providence Institute for Savings, 1929, 1931, 1939, 1944.

McLoughlin, William G. *Rhode Island: A History*. New York: W.W. Norton and Company, 1978.

Newport Mercury, 1759.

SELECTED BIBLIOGRAPHY

O'Neil, Richard, ed. *Patrick O'Brian's Navy: The Illustrated Companion to Jack Aubrey's World*. Philadelphia: Running Press, 2003.

Providence Gazette and Country Journal, 1762.

Rappleye, Charles. *Sons of Providence: The Brown Brothers, the Slave Trade, and the American Revolution*. New York: Simon and Schuster, 2006.

Staples, William R. *The Documentary History of the Destruction of the* Gaspee. Providence, RI: Knowles, Vose, and Anthony, 1845.

Stiles, Ezra. *The Literary Diary of Ezra Stiles, DD, LLD, President of Yale College*. Edited by Franklin Bowditch Dexter. New York: Charles Scribner's Sons, 1901.

Wolf, Stephanie Grauman. *As Various as Their Land: The Everyday Lives of Eighteenth-Century Americans*. Fayetteville: University of Arkansas Press, 2000.

www.gaspee.org

ABOUT THE AUTHOR

Rory Raven is a mentalist who performs at colleges, clubs, corporations and private events throughout the United States. He offers fantastic mind-reading shows and lectures on esoteric subjects. When not on the road, he conducts the Providence Ghost Walk, the original ghosts and graveyards walking tour through the haunted history of Providence, Rhode Island, where

Photo by Judith Reilly.

he makes his home with his wife and various animals. He is the author of three previous books: *Haunted Providence: Strange Tales from the Smallest State*; *Wicked Conduct: The Minister, the Mill Girl and the Murder that Captivated Old Rhode Island*; and *The Dorr War: Treason, Rebellion and the Fight for Reform in Rhode Island*, all available from The History Press. For more information, visit www.roryraven.com.

Visit us at
www.historypress.net